ICONIC

Magazine Covers

The Inside Stories Told by the People

Who Made Them

by **Ian Birch**

FIREFLY BOOKS

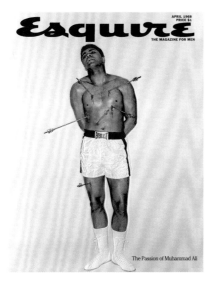

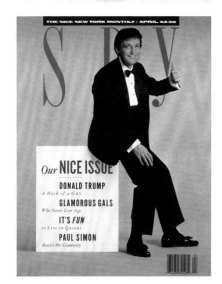

CONTENTS

FOREWORD

ANNE FULENWIDER

I first met Ian Birch while sitting in a cramped office on the 34th floor of the Hearst Tower in New York, when I was executive editor of *Marie Claire* under Joanna Coles (now chief content officer at Hearst), and a small group of us had been charged with improving the magazine's covers. Ian was brought in as a specialist, having launched several groundbreaking magazines in the UK – *Grazia*, *Red*, *Heat* and *Closer* – and was introduced, more or less, as the Irish cover-whisperer.

Typically, our covers had been worked on by three or four of us who crowded around our design director's desk, lobbing ideas for coverlines at the besieged creative director Suzanne Sykes, who was charged with translating our gibberish into something that both made sense and looked striking. These meetings were in stark contrast to my former place of employment, *Vanity Fair*, where Graydon Carter would gather ten or so of us in a wood-panelled conference room with that month's cover projected onto a large screen. The room was so grand that many of us were too intimidated to speak. The *Marie Claire* cover meetings were much more casual, spontaneous and conducive to creative thought, but still, we'd been stuck in the weeds. Ian's perspective, far as he was from our core audience of American women aged 21–35, was of an outsider, albeit with vast magazine experience. Which is why he was so effectively able to remind us of what we were there to do, no matter what our subject matter: create an immediate, emotional impact.

The great covers do this within the first milliseconds of eye contact. The image is arresting, the words complementary, but, most of all, a cultural moment is distilled to its essence. I remember exactly where I was, as I'm guessing many of us do, when I first saw the 1991 image of Demi Moore, naked and pregnant, and the 2015 reveal of Caitlyn Jenner's transgender identity, both on the covers of *Vanity Fair*. Yes, the impact of these covers can be deconstructed and explained, and their geneses were highly orchestrated – months of wooing a subject, of negotiations and collaboration between photographer, stylist, publicist and subject, hours of preparation on set to get just the right light, angle, and expression – and that's weeks before those gruelling hours of coverline brainstorms. A lot can go wrong. Which is why the perfect mix of elements is so elusive – and sometimes comes about accidentally. In the end the most successful covers give the illusion of having been produced by magic.

At my isolated boarding school in New Hampshire, far away from the buzzy world I longed to join, magazines were passed around like contraband in prison, and pored over for hours on end in our dorm rooms – missives from that impossibly glamorous world of New York City. Every page, every ad, every scent strip was analyzed for social codes and clues on how to be sophisticated. (To this day if I ever come across the scent of Giorgio Beverly Hills perfume I am immediately taken back to a freezing cold dorm room in the mid-1980s.)

I finally landed in New York, and gained a foothold in the world I had dreamed of. I've worked at four magazines, produced about 50 covers and led countless coverlines meetings, all in search of that magic alchemy. A lot has happened since I got here. When I landed at *Vanity Fair*, Madonna was on the cover, having given her first interview after the birth of Lourdes, and Bill Clinton's affair with Monica Lewinsky had just been outed by the Drudge Report. The internet had already begun its takeover of our attention spans. And yet, since then, as I'm reminded by Ian and his book, some of the most resonant cultural moments (as well as some of the just plain fun ones) have belonged to magazine covers. As Instagram takes over our lives and fake news spreads like wildfire across social media, I am forever grateful for magazines and their covers – beacons of culture, beaming light across the plains.

Anne Fulenwider is editor-in-chief of American *Marie Claire*

INTRODUCTION

IAN BIRCH

As a teenager in 1960s Belfast, I fell in love with magazines. They introduced me to a community outside of family and school. They taught me about words and pictures, how to structure and present an idea. They were seductive and aspirational. Especially potent was *The Sunday Times Magazine*, a weekly comet of colour and discovery. I remember seeing *Rolling Stone* for the first time in a Belfast boutique in 1968 while wondering if I could afford a Ben Sherman shirt. It was a revelation, a voice for a cultural shift which I only hazily understood but knew I wanted to be part of. I bought the magazine, not the shirt. Little did I realize that its co-founder, Jann Wenner, would be my boss 24 years later.

Like any business, a magazine's first job is to make money for the owner, and that's traditionally done through a combination of advertising and copy sales. The newsstand cover is obviously crucial here: it's the most important marketing tool. It follows that a successful cover is one that sells as many copies as it can to its intended audience. The publishing industry has spent millions over the decades on research, trying to find the magic cover formula. Some titles have come very close, like *People*, whose covers have been calibrated with forensic brilliance. But even *People* can trip up.

The received thinking goes something like this. A mainstream cover should be instantly recognizable under the 5/5 rule (we make our choice within five seconds from five feet away); it should have an attractive and accessible photograph with strong eye contact (we read the picture before the text and we prefer photography to illustration or pure type because it takes less time and effort to decode); it should have an easily digestible and relatable mix of cover lines that pepper the expected with the odd surprise (anything depressing like a tragedy should be wrapped up in empathy); it should have a tone of warm, light banter (somewhere between a pun and a punch line); and one of the dominant colours should be "buy-me" red. Don't get me wrong: to work within these commercial diktats and produce a cover that crackles *and* sells well is an enviable skill. Over the last 40 years, I have been lucky enough to work with designers and writers who have pulled this off.

But the covers here are different. I didn't choose them on the basis of sales – their newsstand numbers fluctuated between the dismal and the dynamic. I chose them because they broke boundaries and started conversations. They made a moment feel red-hot and meaningful. Some confronted taboos about race and sex. Some ridiculed hypocrisy. Some memorialized a catastrophic event. Some provided a voice that was absent from the mainstream. Some were rallying calls.

Some bordered on the crude. Some turned design conventions upside down. Some ended up hanging in galleries, such as George Lois's *Esquire* covers, exhibited in New York's MoMA in 2008.

They are social documents with unique backstories. I wanted to hear these stories from the creative mavericks behind them – the editor, the art director, the writer, the photographer, the photography director, the cartoonist, the stylist, the publisher and, occasionally, the celebrity or a relevant academic. That's why I start in the late 1950s; prior to this, key players are sadly either dead or unavailable. I end when covers were re-energized by the twin political thunderbolts of Brexit and Trump, and the warp speed of the political news cycle. These covers became more adversarial because they could and should.

As I write, there is an overwhelming sense that the post-World War II magazine era is ending. The internet has taken over as the engine of popular culture and, in the process, decimated the print business model. Revenues from advertising and circulation have been shrinking rapidly, and that has forced legacy companies to cut staff, close, combine or sell some titles and reduce the frequencies of others, invest – often belatedly and furiously – in digital, video and voice-enabled services, and search for other ways to monetize their still-sizeable subscriber files. It's a grim landscape, especially as platform monopolies like Google and Facebook suck up all the oxygen and most of the digital advertising money. And, like the entertainment and tech industries, publishing is facing an increasing number of sexual misconduct allegations, notably in high-end fashion photography. On the bright side, there has been a surge in the independent sector of handsomely designed niche titles, but as yet their commercial pulling power is limited. With technology, the barriers to producing magazines have never been lower, but the barriers to making them successful have never been higher.

And what of the future for magazines? Will they devolve further into marketing add-ons, stylish but supine? Like American public radio, will they ask their audiences for funding through a mix of subscription, membership fees and donation drives? Will they take a similar path to vinyl, which now enjoys a retro prestige? Kurt Andersen, astute social observer, former editor of *New York* and co-founder of *Spy*, hits the nail on the head: "Eventually, they'll become like sailboats," he said. "They don't need to exist anymore. But people will still love them, and make them and buy them."[1]

1 Quoted in Sydney Ember and Michael M Grynbaum, "The Not-So-Glossy Future of Magazines", *The New York Times*, 23 September 2017.

LATE
1950s

one

AUGUST 1958

FIFTY CENTS

THE HOMOSEXUAL VIEWPOINT

I am glad I am homo-sexual

D.F.

ONE

AUGUST 1958

Managing editor: Don Slater

Art director: Eve Elloree

Cover artist: Dawn Fredericks

Craig M Loftin is Lecturer in American
    Studies at California State University,
    Fullerton.[1]

In 1953, when McCarthyism raged, the United States' first openly gay magazine was launched on newsstands across the country.

CRAIG M LOFTIN:

Keep in mind that the Alfred Kinsey reports had come out. Everyone knew who Kinsey was. I mean he was on the cover of *Time* magazine. Kinsey's *Sexual Behavior in the Human Male*, in 1948, said that over a third of American men had had same-sex contacts. And he says, very bluntly, there is no reason to have laws against it. Now that's one of the big things that helped inspire the homophile movement. *One* came out of that political movement. This was not a magazine for leisure and fun. The underlying idea was to bring all gay people together as "one".

They were hoping that heterosexuals might pick up the magazine and flip through its contents and overcome their own prejudices. They would mail it to prominent judges, politicians and famous writers like Tennessee Williams, Gore Vidal and Norman Mailer.

Two-thirds of the magazine's 3,000–5,000 monthly readers preferred buying their copies at newsstands, largely because they were fearful of being on a subscription list that might get seized by police. Newsstand visibility, therefore, was an important factor in the magazine's national proliferation. *One*'s artists and editors had to fashion a visual style on the covers that would evoke gayness in a recognizable way, yet avoid inciting backlash from postal authorities, vice squads or censorship groups.[2]

Most of the illustrations were drawn by two women who were a couple. A commercial artist named Joan Corbin drew under the pseudonym Eve Elloree during the 1950s, and in the 1960s Dawn Fredericks took over most of Corbin's duties. This represented a rare example of female creative control within a male-dominated homophile organization.

There was a growing frustration from them and other women that they were not getting heard, and eventually a lot of them ended up leaving *One* and joining the Daughters of Bilitis, which was the first lesbian organization. They had their own magazine called *The Ladder* (*see* Figure 1), which started in 1956 and was modelled off of *One* basically.

Their illustrations were non-threatening, and non-threatening is a key concept here. These homophile organizations of the 1950s were very assimilationist organizations. They wanted to be accepted by society. Kind of like the black Civil Rights Movement in its earlier phases. You dress nice, you speak professionally, you win over the mainstream by showing them how patriotic and American and normal you are.

What's striking about this cover is how big the words are – huge letters proclaiming that in a shocking, daring way. But it's not some menacing image. I would describe it as a prideful stoicism that says, "I have a right to exist."

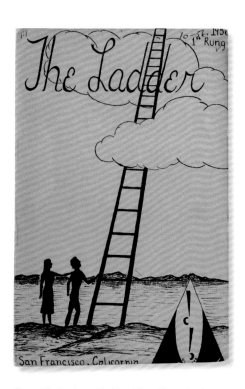

Figure 1 *The first issue of the United States' first national lesbian magazine,* The Ladder.

---

1 Craig M Loftin is the author of *Masked Voices: Gay Men and Lesbians in Cold War America* (SUNY Press, 2012) and *Letters to One: Gay and Lesbian Voices from the 1950s and 1960s* (SUNY Press, 2012).

2 C Loftin, "Drawing Attention: The Ambiguous Artwork of America's First Gay Magazine", paper presented at the Pacific Coast Branch of the American Historical Association Conference, San Diego 2012. Reproduced with kind permission of the author.

THE QUEEN

15 SEPTEMBER 1959

Editor-in-chief: Jocelyn Stevens

Editor: Beatrix Miller

Art editor: Mark Boxer

Associate editors: Quentin Crewe,
Drusilla Beyfus

Cover credit: "Photographed at the
Gargoyle by Desmond Russell."

Jocelyn Stevens bought *The Queen* for around £10,000 in 1957 as a 25th birthday present to himself. He immediately set about turning the genteel high-society fortnightly (launched in 1861) into a graphically innovative and sharper-tongued vehicle for the new generation of talent. He recruited Mark Boxer, his compatriot from Cambridge, as art director and Tony Armstrong-Jones, who would become Lord Snowden, as photographer. Stevens had such a volcanic temper that *Private Eye* nicknamed him "Piranha Teeth". Stories abounded of him tussling with staff in the office, firing people on a whim, throwing typewriters out of windows and terminating telephone calls by cutting the cord with a pair of scissors. He later told Sue Lawley on *Desert Island Discs*[1] that most of the stories were true.

This cover toasted the consumer "boom", the feature opening with "When did you last hear the word austerity? Nearly two thousand million pounds is pouring out of pockets and wallets and handbags and changing into air tickets and oysters, television sets and caviar, art treasures and vacuum cleaners, cigars and refrigerators."[2] Stevens later wrote: "It was our 'you've never had it so good'[3] issue and the Prime Minister liked the message. Reggie Maudling, who was Chancellor of the Exchequer, told me later that Harold Macmillan had arranged at the Cabinet meeting the following day for every Cabinet Minister to have a copy of the magazine in front of him. None of which stopped us attacking some of his Cabinet appointments following his election victory a month later."[4]

DRUSILLA BEYFUS:

The Queen was a class effort in every respect. The editorial mix was unlike anything else in its canon, combining sharp social observation, tiptop art direction and photography and pieces by literary stars.

Private jokes were allowed in print. A goat-footsure touch on the slippery slopes of social class distinction characterized the comment features, such as a witty survey of The Establishment[5] and a tilt at the machinations of newspaper gossip columnists. Literary lions counted. Among others, I recall pieces by James Thurber, Colin MacInnes, Penelope Gilliatt, Victoria Sackville-West, Clement Freud, Elizabeth Jane Howard.

We found a bifocal way of reflecting an upper-crust world, seeing things from the viewpoint of a bona fide paid-up member of the elite, and from a modern outsider's perspective.

The Boom cover is a great example of Mark Boxer's touch in combining images with cover-lines to put over the whole atmosphere of a story. The issue in every way represented a glamorous benchmark on the (temporary) end of national austerity.

1   *Desert Island Discs*, first broadcast 8 March 1992.
2   Condensed from *The Queen*, 15 September 1959, p.29.
3   Harold Macmillan's famous soundbite from a speech he delivered at a Tory rally on 20 July 1957 in Bedford.
4   *The Sixties in Queen*, edited by Nicholas Coleridge and Stephen Quinn, Ebury Press, 1987, pp.10–11.
5   "The Establishment Chronicle", *The Queen*, August 1959.

TWEN

OCTOBER 1959 AND 20 APRIL 1960

Editor-in-chief: Adolf Theobald

Picture editing and layout: Willy Fleckhaus

DECEMBER 1964 AND JUNE 1966

Art director: Willy Fleckhaus

Assistant to art director: Christian Diener

Managing editor: Willi Herzog

Assistant art director (1964–6):
   Will Hopkins[1]

Anna von Munchhausen is content director
   at Die Zeit newspaper.

Germany had not seen a magazine like *Twen* before. Launched in Cologne in 1959, it spoke directly to the liberal post-war twentysomething generation (the name was an abbreviation of the English word "twenty"[2]). It championed pop culture, questioned society, looked outward to the United States and Britain and espoused sexuality in a big, sometimes profligate way. The design, by Willy Fleckhaus, introduced a radical 12-column grid together with a startling use of photography (contrasting large and small pictures) and typography (bold headlines with Brutalist-like slabs of text that cared more about design than meaning). Fleckhaus's influence was enormous.

Design critic Klaus Thomas Edelman believes that many of Fleckhaus's designs "express his continual attempts to make a fresh start for himself. A friend, Adolf Theobald, explains: 'Drafted by Hitler into the armed forces, and cheated out of his youth, Fleckhaus used graphics to relive the youth that he had been denied: protest, opposition, liberalism, sentimentality, pleasure – all these things were worked out, processed through the layout.'"[3]

ANNA VON MUNCHHAUSEN:

I fell in love with *Twen* in the mid-1960s as a boarding-school girl in Germany. Don't forget that it was a child of the late Adenauer[4] years: a chancellor over 80 years old led the country. Germany was busy forgetting Hitler and wanted to rebuild the nation – the *Wirtschaftswunder*[5] – without being told what role the Germans played from 1933 to 1945. The younger generation felt that under the surface there was much emotional repression in their parents' minds.

To read *Twen* meant you were a member of an urban young elite, enjoying life, enjoying free love and feeling optimistic about the future. It was a sort of guideline to what was hip. It invented a certain female role model: positive thinking, independent sexiness which was completely new to German women. Willy Fleckhaus invented the position of art director in Germany.

WILL HOPKINS:

When I first saw *Twen*, I loved it and decided that I was going to work for Fleckhaus. I'd say to people, the Lord told me I had to go to Germany. My wife

twen

Köln   Oktober 1959   Heft Nr. 3   Preis 1.– DM   Österreich S. 8.–   Schweiz sfr. 1.–

ICH SEHE
NETTE MÄDCHEN
GERN

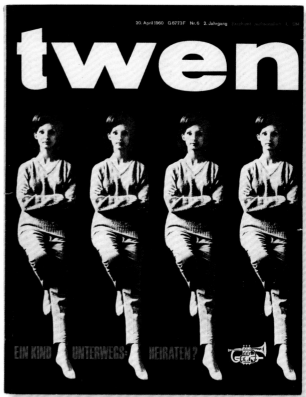

twen

20. April 1960   G 6773 F   Nr. 6   2. Jahrgang

EIN KIND   UNTERWEGS: HEIRATEN?

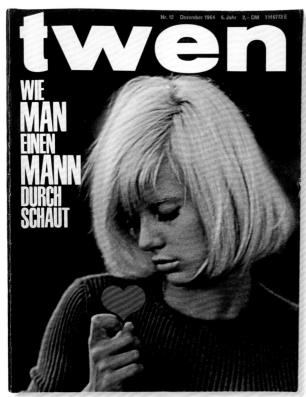

twen

Nr. 12   Dezember 1964   6. Jahr   2.– DM   1 H 6773 E

WIE
MAN
EINEN
MANN
DURCH
SCHAUT

twen

Nr. 6   Juni 1966   8. Jahr   2.20 DM   1 H 6773 E

Der neue Report über das Tabu der lesbischen Liebe

Warum manche Mädchen
nur Mädchen lieben

and I were living in Chicago where I was working for Chess Records. Six months later, we were in Cologne.

I went to their office but Fleckhaus was on vacation. They said, give us your phone number, but I didn't have one so I went back every day and sat on their couch. One day, they got into trouble with a deadline so I started pasting up. I ended up spending two years there.

The cover would be arrived at very quickly. The black background, a picture of a beautiful woman, a provocative cover line and sometimes something a little ornamental by someone like Heinz Edelmann.[6] The trumpet was just an ornament.

Fleckhaus never had to justify what he was doing. Most of the time, when we did a cover, the editor was nowhere to be found. It was his magazine, not the editor's. He was very emotional about the way he chose pictures. We'd project slides on the wall and he'd say, take that out, take that out, take that out: very rapid, very intuitive.

One of my favourites is the Sylvie Vartan[7] cover [below left]. It was the first thing I saw Fleckhaus and Diener work on together. That cover expressed the German notion of romance and the sentimentality that they seemed to love.

1   Will Hopkins went on to art-direct magazines including *Look*, *GEO* and *American Photographer*.
2   Sourced from Steven Heller, "The Modern Master of Magazine Design", *Graphis* magazine, no. 249, vol. 43 (May/June 1987), p.10.
3   Klaus Thomas Edelmann, "Paint It Black", *Eye* magazine, no. 3, vol. 1 (Spring 1991). Reproduced with the kind permission of *Eye*. Article available at: *http://www.eyemagazine.com/feature/article/paint-it-black*. Adolf Theobald was a co-founder of *Twen*.
4   Konrad Adenauer, first chancellor of the Federal Republic of Germany (West Germany), 1949–63.
5   The "Economic Miracle", also known as the "Miracle on the Rhein", describes the rapid reconstruction and development of the economies of West Germany and Austria after World War II.
6   Regular illustrator for *Twen* throughout the Sixties who also art-directed the Beatles' *Yellow Submarine* film.
7   December 1964. Vartan is a French singer who was at the forefront of the yé-yé pop sound in the 1960s.

1960s

man
about town

January 1961   2/6   50¢   Cheat the cold

Raze the boom-towns

Read Lawrence Durrell   Live it rich

Drink champagne   Get wise to Europe

ABOUT TOWN

JANUARY 1961
SEPTEMBER 1961

Publishers: Clive Labovitch,
    Michael Heseltine
Editor: David Hughes
Art director: Thomas Wolsey
Photography for both covers:
    Terence Donovan
Art assistant: Jeanette Collins

Michael Heseltine and Clive Labovitch, freshly graduated from Oxford, set up Cornmarket Press[1] and bought their first magazine, the "undistinguished quarterly"[2] *Man About Town*, in 1959. They turned it into a sleek, sharp-witted and influential men's monthly, shortening the name to *About Town* in late January 1961 (and then *Town* in February 1962). As Heseltine later noted, Labovitch's "inspired decision was to recruit Tom Wolsey as art director"[3] from the prestigious Crawford's Advertising Agency.

JEANETTE COLLINS:

Tom was born in Germany and had a singular German accent that Peter Sellers learned for *Dr Strangelove*. He was slim, small and dapper with little hands – sort of perfect in every detail. He was like a little gremlin. I don't think I had a real conversation with him until years after I left *Town*. Everything was about work. He was amazing but at times impossible.

I remember one major fight which went on all day between Heseltine, Labovitch and the editor Nick Tomalin about where to crop the nipple on the fragmented mirrors cover.[4] As modest as that cover is, it caused absolute mayhem. Tom wanted the nipple in, and Michael said, "Over my dead body." Eventually, the nipple was cropped. *Town* had always distanced itself from any sort of soft porn-y covers and I would say here that Tom was putting a tentative toe into the permissive Sixties. When he lost, he went back to his office. Outside his door were the coat racks. He took down Nick Tomalin's coat, dropped it on the floor and jumped up and down on it. Then he picked it up very delicately, hung it back up and went, "Tee hee hee." That was the kind of relationship there was with editors.

The magic was done when you weren't there. Tom would come in late in the mornings and would go out early for a long lunch, returning at 4pm. He then shut himself in his office and worked late into the night. I would arrive in the morning to a pile of layouts to prepare for the printer.

I once wrote this about him: "Tom used typography as mortar to bond image and word. He did overprint a good deal, but far from destroying the image he often heightened its effect by using the type to echo angles within the picture, to emphasize a visual point, to create excitement or reinforce a mood."[5] One cover that sums this up is "The Balloon" where the type anticipates what the photograph couldn't – the balloon's explosion. And, by the way, that's Tom's hand – delicate and hairy.

Tom was always looking for "shock tactics", and the "new breed" of photographers such as David Bailey, John Bulmer, Donovan, Duffy and Don McCullin provided this. The "Anatomy of Anger" cover was a black-and-white photograph of Chita Rivera[6] by Donovan, but Tom gave it a graphic treatment to emphasize the mood with this hot-orange background, and the shocking-pink lightning flash at the bottom. The grainy effect was achieved at the developing and printmaking stage, and the artwork for the flash was supplied as an overlay. The result was a tightly designed explosion of anger.

1 According to Wikipedia, "The partners split in 1965, with Heseltine renaming his half of the business Haymarket Press to publish *Management Today*." https://en.wikipedia.org/wiki/Haymarket_Media_Group
2 Michael Heseltine quoted in "Haymarket 50 Years: 50 Glorious Moments", *Campaign*, 26 October 2007. http://www.campaignlive.co.uk/article/haymarket-50-years-50-glorious-moments-1-2/763156#z4uz4eeoFKzQ0Uqv.99
3 Ibid.
4 May 1962, "Facets of the Daily Mirror".
5 Jeanette Collins, "*Town* and Tom Wolsey", in *British Photography, 1955–1965: The Master Craftsmen in Print*, The Photographers' Gallery, London, 1983, p.10.
6 American actress who was starring in the smash-hit musical *Bye Bye Birdie* in London.

2/6 60¢   September 1961

about town

Anatomy of anger
Test match fever
Upheaval in politics
Lightning fighters
Shoot your own film

EROS

AUTUMN 1962

Editor and publisher: Ralph Ginzburg

Art director: Herb Lubalin

Associate editors: Warren Boroson,
   Susan Ginzburg

Cover photography: Bert Stern

Eros was a sumptuous half-book, half-magazine with a large format (13 × 10in), hardback covers and no advertising. The subject matter was the erotic, and Marilyn was the third cover, her last studio portraits which Bert Stern had taken six weeks before her death and published for the first time here, six weeks after it.

Ginzburg wrote an illuminating editor's note: "The scratches and orange crosses on many of the photographs on the cover and following pages are not defects. They were made by Marilyn Monroe herself, her own reactions to various shots that showed a strand of hair out of place or a pose she felt was somehow awkward. We thought her markings were so interesting that we decided to leave them in."[1]

SHOSHANA (FORMERLY SUSAN) GINZBURG:

Eros was entirely my idea. I was just a kid when we started that – 19 or 20. Ralph always wanted to publish a magazine, and I had just finished taking a course about Freud which called eros the life force. So I said to Ralph, "Everything is about sex so why don't we do a magazine about eros?" I didn't say, "Why don't we call it Eros." He said, "What would we put in there?" and I said, "Anything because everything is related to it. It gives us a lot of freedom while giving us a hook." The girly magazines like *Playboy*, *Dude* and *Nugget* were doing well then. Ours would be nothing like that: ours would be clean and classy, from day one. Full of joy and art.

Ralph knew Herb was the best designer in the world so we got him. The square format gave him so much more visual leeway that other magazines didn't have. We used a special printing method called flame set lithography which gave a vibrancy to the colour.

We knew Bert Stern. In those days, people had trouble getting anything published that showed nudity but wasn't trash. There was no handsome place to put that kind of art. That's why Bert wanted us because he knew what our attitude would be: honest and respectful. It was a collaboration between Bert and Herb, whose layouts made the pictures sing. Bert took such a loving view of Marilyn and even saved the negatives where she "x-ed" out the contact sheets. She did it in such a violent way like she was saying, "Make it gone." They looked too much like the way she thought she really was. Such self-hatred. She was a terrific actress but Marilyn isn't who she was. She was Norma Jean. We honoured her with this. It was our tribute.

1 *Eros*, Autumn 1962, p.5.

EROS

On June 21, 1962, Bert Stern took the last studio portraits of Marilyn Monroe. That was six weeks before her tragic death. A portfolio of these photographs begins on page three.

December 1963 Price One Dollar

Esquire
The magazine for Men

ESQUIRE

From 1962 to 1972, Madison Avenue art director George Lois and American *Esquire* editor Harold Hayes created some of the most original, ideas-rich, uncompromising and incendiary covers in magazine history. Lois often worked with photographer Carl Fischer, Lois creating the concept, drawing a tight sketch of each (Figures 2–5) and directing them, and then Fischer bringing it to life. "People would say to me, 'You got some balls doing those covers.' I would say, 'No, it's Harold who has the balls.' There's no editor in the world who would do that now – allow me to choose the article in the upcoming issue, and then accept each cover I created with appreciation and pleasure."[1]

DECEMBER 1963
Editor: Harold T P Hayes
Cover design: George Lois
Cover photography: Carl Fischer

Hayes asked Lois to do a "Christmassy" cover for December 1963. "Sonny Liston was perfect for the part," Lois later explained. "By now he was known by everyone as the meanest man in the world. He had served time for armed robbery and didn't give a damn about his image."[2] Lois didn't add Liston's name to the cover. It wasn't a story about the world-champion boxer, it was an image of a black Santa Claus.

GEORGE LOIS:
Harold understood that I was making a strong remark and it would be very controversial. A lot of liberals were pissed with the cover but he defended it big time. When Cassius Clay saw it, and he knew Liston was a convicted criminal, he said, "George, that's the last black motherfucker America wants to see coming down their chimney."

I couldn't go to Vegas for the shoot because I was directing TV spots in New York that week. I arranged for the photography of Liston by having Joe Louis, who was relegated to being a "greeter" at a casino, bring Liston into the room where Fischer was going to take the photographs. I knew Liston would cave in to Joe. Liston was a badass, but thought Joe Louis was a god. Louis told Liston that it would be fun to wear the Santa hat on a magazine cover.

Harold said that was the cover that really made *Esquire*, and he wasn't talking about the money or sales. Let me quote you what he wrote about it: "In the national climate of 1963, thick with racial fear, Lois's angry icon insisted on several things: the split in our culture was showing; the notion of racial equality was a bad joke; the felicitations of this season – goodwill to all men, etc – carried irony more than sentiment."[3]

There was a lot of hate mail but the culture understood it. *Time* magazine said it was "one of the greatest social statements of the plastic arts since Picasso's *Guernica*". Years later, there was an article in *Adweek* which talked about how that cover cost the magazine $750,000. They lost a lot of clients, all Southern accounts, a lot of Southern textile mills. Harold wasn't perturbed.

CARL FISCHER:

Sonny was living in Las Vegas at the time so I went out there with Christmas gear: the hat, the jacket. I set up something in the hotel room. He said, "Forget it. I'm not putting on any fucking Santa Claus hat."

By coincidence, and this was our good luck and not our wit, the hotel manager came by with his daughter, a cute little girl. Sonny liked her. The two of them started playing together, so I said, "Let's take a picture of her with the Santa Claus hat on." So I did and then I said, "Let's take a picture of the two of you together." He put his arm around her; she put her arm around him. I said, "That's great. Let's put the hat on you, Sonny, just for one shot." He said, "All right, goddammit." We had the picture.

I can never understand why people do these things. Sonny must have realized when he put on the hat and the little girl was pushed off camera but he didn't say anything. Maybe he was confused. Maybe he didn't realize. Maybe we did trick him. I don't know.

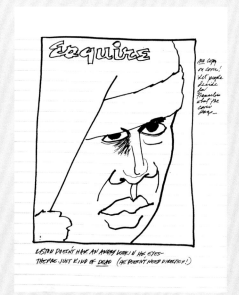

Figure 2 George Lois's preparatory sketch.

1 Interview with Ian Birch.
2 "The First Black Santa", in George Lois, *The Esquire Covers @MoMA*, Assouline, 2009, p. 56.
3 "Harold Hayes on George Lois and those Esquire Covers", ibid., p.25.

Editor: Harold T P Hayes
Cover design: George Lois

On 25 October 1965[1] John Sack, who had served in Korea and was then a writer and producer at CBS in New York, sent Harold Hayes a brilliant story idea. He wanted to tell "the true story" of a military unit as it moved from basic training in Fort Dix, New Jersey, to first combat in Vietnam. He wanted to portray the soldiers with all their doubts, fears and dreams as faithfully and comprehensively as he could. Sack was shaping the role of the embedded war reporter.

Hayes gave the go-ahead and the following January Sack was detailed to M company. He went with them to Saigon and soon "the incident happened". [2] A cavalryman, hearing voices from inside a bunker, told one of M company to throw a grenade into it. The grenade exploded and "ten or a dozen women and children came shrieking out in their crinkled pajamas; no blood, no apparent injuries, though...Then another soldier, 'a specialist', peered into the remains and cried 'Oh my God!' A second specialist shouted, 'What's the matter?' 'They hit a little girl' and in his muscular black arms the first specialist carried out a seven-year-old, long black hair and little earrings, staring eyes – eyes, her eyes are what froze themselves onto M's memory, it seemed there was no white to those eyes, nothing but black ellipses like black goldfish."[3]

A whopping 33,000 words, it's the longest story Esquire has ever published and has become a benchmark in the history of New Journalism and war reporting.

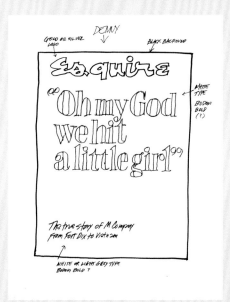

Figure 3 George Lois's preparatory sketch.

1 Sourced from Carol Polsgrove, *It Wasn't Pretty, Folks, But Didn't We Have Fun? Surviving the '60s with Esquire's Harold Hayes*, RDR Books, 2001, p.148.
2 John Sack, 'M', *Esquire*, October 1966.
3 Ibid.

GEORGE LOIS:

I had a cover about to go to press, and I swear I don't remember what it was. I usually didn't have the actual written piece in my hand on anything I worked on because I had to give them art two months ahead – beats me why. But when Hayes sent me John Sack's story, I perused through the pages and that quote punched me in the mouth. I called Hayes and said, "Kill the cover I did. I'll have a new one for you in three, four hours." I sent him it. He called me up and said, "Oh my God".

It was my chance to inform America that, similar to the Korean war, we were committing yet another act of genocide. The cover appeared when "only" 6,000 GIs had died. The stark design screamed to the world that something was wrong, terribly wrong. American boys, with mind-numbing hatred of the "gooks" – an insult used by most GIs in the Korean and Vietnam wars – were fighting in another brutally immoral, racist war.

AUGUST 1966
PRICE 75c

Esquire

THE MAGAZINE FOR MEN

"Oh my God –we hit a little girl."

The true story of M Company. From Fort Dix to Vietnam.

APRIL 1968
PRICE $1

Esquire

THE MAGAZINE FOR MEN

The Passion of Muhammad Ali

APRIL 1968

Editor: Harold T P Hayes

Cover design: George Lois

Cover photography: Carl Fischer

In 1967 Cassius Clay, the world's heavyweight champion, converted to Islam under the tutelage of Elijah Muhammad, taking the name Muhammad Ali. "When Ali refused military service as a conscientious objector because of his new religion, a federal jury sentenced him to five years in jail for draft evasion," wrote Lois later. "Boxing commissions then stripped him of his title and denied him the right to fight."[1] Lois decided to pose Ali as a contemporary St Sebastian, after the 15th-century painting by Francesco Botticini in which the body is pierced by six arrows. St Sebastian was a martyr for his religious beliefs; so, argued Lois, was Ali.

Kurt Andersen calls this "the greatest cover ever created, making a political statement without being grim or stupid or predictable. It's not just a great idea, but visually elegant, economical, perfect."[2]

CARL FISCHER:

Ali arrived alone, as I remember. In those days, people were famous, but they were not unapproachable. They weren't surrounded by people taking care of them like today. I had the arrows made and practised with them. When you're doing a symbol, the only thing you really want to show is the symbol. You don't need a background. The focus was on the arrows. The design was the thing itself as so many good covers are: simple, direct statements.

GEORGE LOIS:

I told Ali to bring his pretty white shoes and trunks. I showed him a postcard photograph of St Sebastian. I chose it because it's one where the body is strong and simple and the head's in agony. I said, "Muhammad, I want you to pose like this." He said, "George, this cat's a Christian. I can't pose as a saint." Elijah Muhammad was in Chicago so we got him on the phone. Ali explained what we were going to do and then put me on. He wanted to know if I was a churchgoing Christian. I said, absolutely. Greek Orthodox, the mother church. Finally, he said he thought it would be a wonderful image. Phew ...

CARL FISCHER:

We had a technical problem: the arrows didn't stay horizontal when we pasted them on. They hung down, so even though it was a very simple idea, the solution was very complex. I hung a horizontal bar above Ali and from that we hung monofilament cables, fishing wire, very thin, very light, to keep the arrows in place. That forced Ali to stand still for a half an hour. Fortunately, he didn't play his celebrity, and it was fine. He was a very funny guy, very impressive and very gracious. He saw the problem that we had.

GEORGE LOIS:

When we had attached the arrows, Ali pointed to each one and said, "Hey George, Lyndon Johnson, General Westmoreland, Clark Clifford, Hubert Humphrey, Robert McNamara and Dean Rusk." I almost fainted. It was the best thing I ever heard.

When the cover came out, it was hated by everybody but the young people who were subject to the draft. When a man like him, who couldn't be more manly or more spiritual, can come out against the war, and risk going to jail for five years, it gave millions of young people courage. He went on a crazy college tour where he would do a kind of one-hour talk, telling funny stories. Not a militant speech but about being a black guy in a white world – where everything's white; where the snow is white; where it's "Snow White and the Seven Dwarves". He had this whole schtick. The kids would go crazy.

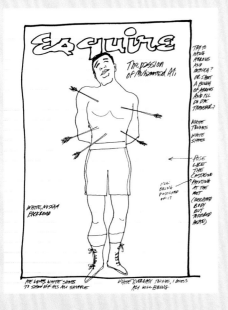

Figure 4 George Lois's preparatory sketch.

1 George Lois, "Proclaiming the Martyrdom of Muhammad Ali for Refusing to Fight in a Bad War", in $ellebrity, Phaidon, 2003.
2 Quoted by Lois on his website: http://www.georgelois. com/ali-as-st.-sebastian.html

MAY 1969

Editor: Harold T P Hayes

Cover design: George Lois

Cover photography: Carl Fischer

"An *Esquire* cover of me drowning in a can of Campbell's soup? I love it! But George, aren't you gonna have to build a giant can of soup?"[1]

So said Andy Warhol to George Lois when he heard the cover concept. Lois had already done multiple photomontage covers for *Esquire,* but this visual joke – part mocking, part homage – ranks as one of his finest. "You could look at it as just funny, or you look at it as how fame swallows people – the absurdity of fame," he later said. "But he really stood for something. Pop Art was ludicrous to me, but I could see why it was catching on."[2]

CARL FISCHER:

The basic shot was a soup can with the dirty lid open a certain amount so that we could get the logo in. I spent the day dropping children's marbles, one by one, into the soup. We did a million splashes and finally got one that made a nice hole to drop Andy into.

I photographed Warhol a lot. His mother and he lived up the block from me on Lexington. He would do anything to be on a cover of a magazine – and for no money. He ran an ad once in *The Village Voice* saying, "I'm available for endorsing products" for money. We had him come into the studio and said, "You're falling into the ocean, just about to drown and you're dying." We did a whole bunch of pictures of him with his arms up, his arms out, screaming, whatever. George sent it out to a retoucher and they put the two shoots together.

Figure 5 George Lois's preparatory sketch.

1   Quoted in George Lois, *The Esquire Covers @ MoMA*, Assouline, 2009, p.134.
2   Condensed from Alex Hoyt, "The Story Behind the Iconic Andy Warhol 'Esquire' Cover", the *Atlantic*, 7 June 2012.

MAY 1969
PRICE $1

Esquire

THE MAGAZINE FOR MEN

The final decline and total collapse
of the American avant-garde.

PRIVATE EYE

5 FEBRUARY 1965
1963 ANNUAL
Editor: Richard Ingrams
Cover artist: Gerald Scarfe

Gerald Scarfe hit the spotlight in 1963 with a drawing inside *Private Eye* of Prime Minister Harold Macmillan, naked and bosomy on an Arne Jacobsen chair, in a wicked parody of Lewis Morley's famous photograph of Christine Keeler during the Profumo affair. The cartoon became the cover of the magazine's 1963 annual, which WH Smith promptly banned.

GERALD SCARFE:

In the early 1960s cartooning was incredibly bland. I worked for *Punch* where I'd done really typical cartoons of mothers-in-law behind the door with rolling pins waiting for the drunken son-in-law to come home and people on desert islands putting messages in bottles. Then along came *Private Eye* and the so-called satire boom. They just found me, and it was like a refreshing breath of air to be able to tell the truth after the crushingly dull and cloying 1950s.

I really did go for it. I knew when I was making a drawing that it had to be vicious. Richard Ingrams said, "You could always rely on Gerald to do something cutting or nasty." No more desert islands unless they had sharks in them. I realize that I do have this bitter side and it sort of enveloped me. But it seemed to be what I was meant to do.

I began to draw political figures. Macmillan was the first one. Strangely enough, there was an incredible reaction to it. Someone later said that no one since the 18th century had drawn politicians naked – not since Gillray. I was being continually likened to Hogarth, Gillray and Rowlandson[1] – whom, incidentally, I don't in any way draw parallels with or think of myself in the same ilk – but I can see why they said it because there is the same sort of *purpose* behind it. I'm giving my view on society and politics, which is what Gillray and Rowlandson did.

The Times sent me to draw Churchill because it was his last day in Parliament, 27 July 1964. The Sergeant at Arms had to give me special dispensation to draw in the House of Commons because you're not allowed to do that. In those days, we really didn't know what we know about personalities now, especially of that ilk. Churchill was still depicted in the newspapers, the *Daily Express* and so forth, as this bulldog figure, standing on the cliffs of Dover with a cigar defying the Hun with a bowler hat, and Vera Lynn singing in the background. Anyway, he was brought in by two helpers on either side. A shambling wreck of a man,

PRIVATE EYE

No. 82
Friday
5 February 65

1/6

obviously senile: it was an incredible shock. Poor old boy. He just sat there as an empty shell.

What was I supposed to draw? Was I supposed to draw the old bulldog or am I supposed to draw what I see? When I took it back to *The Times* they wouldn't publish it because they said, imagine what Clemmie, his wife, would feel if that came through the letterbox. I remember going to a *Private Eye* lunch that day and I told Peter Cook about it. "Oh, let's have it," he said. No such compunction at all there – bugger all that. So he stuffed it on the cover the week Churchill died and, ironically, it has been recently hanging in the House of Commons. That was a strange drawing for me: not really a caricature in my usual style.

1 William Hogarth (1697–1764), James Gillray (c.1756–1815) and Thomas Rowlandson (1756–1827), pioneers of the satirical cartoon in the UK who made robust use of caricature.

FACT

SEPTEMBER/OCTOBER 1964

Editor and publisher: Ralph Ginzburg

Art director: Herb Lubalin

Contributing editor: Warren Boroson

Staff: Shoshana (formerly Susan) Ginzburg

In January 1964 Ralph Ginzburg launched *Fact*, a black-and-white quarterly he described as a "hell-raising, muckraking magazine of dissent that would try to improve society by bringing data to the fore that was not generally known".[1] Herb Lubalin's stark art direction perfectly framed this content.

The US presidential election would happen in November: Republican Senator Barry M Goldwater was running against incumbent Democrat Lyndon B Johnson. Alarmed by Goldwater's extreme conservative stance, and his advocacy of the use of nuclear weapons, *Fact* felt it had a duty to warn its audience.

It sent a questionnaire to the United States' 12,356 psychiatrists asking, "Do you believe Barry Goldwater is psychologically fit to serve as President of the United States?" Of this number, 2,417 psychiatrists responded and 1,189 said that he was not. The questionnaire left room for "Comments" and "over a quarter of a million words of professional opinion were received".[2]

The comments from the 1,189 pulled no punches about Goldwater's mental fitness and the risks he posed. Goldwater brought a libel action, seeking damages of $1,000,000. The court found against Ginzburg and Boroson. Goldwater was awarded $1.00 in compensatory damages and punitive damages of $75,000.

In response, the American Psychiatric Association issued the so-called "Goldwater rule" in 1973 which made it "unethical for a psychiatrist to offer a professional opinion unless he or she has conducted an examination and has been granted proper authorization for such a statement".[3] This is still in effect as I write in 2018, although some mental health professionals, who question President Trump's psychiatric state, believe that the rule should be revisited because it undermines their "duty to inform".

SHOSHANA GINZBURG:

I was married to Ralph and we were so worried that Goldwater would become president that we made plans to move to New Zealand. We knew he was out of his mind and were very afraid. We were shocked when he sued because he made it all the more public. The trial was amazing. We had a very good lawyer, Harris B Sternberg. He set up a huge blackboard in the courtroom with the article written on it. He went through it, sentence by sentence, and said, "Is this the sentence that offended you?" I was digging my fingernails into my palm not to laugh.

At one point, I was in the elevator alone with Goldwater and I said to him, "You might be surprised to know that you remind me of my dad." He looked at me as if I had stuck a pin in his finger. He didn't know what to do. I'm supposed to be his vile enemy and here am I saying something that might be taken as nice. If I have a chance to calm down an enemy, I'm going to do it.

We never thought there was a chance he would win. Never! We thought America was the land of free speech and it's absolutely basic that the public can question anything about a candidate running for president. We were so wrong. We were faced with huge fines and it eventually put *Fact* out of business.

How could that cover be more on point today?

1   Quoted in Philip B Meggs, "Two Magazines of the Turbulent '60s: A 'Perspective", *Print 48* (March–April 1994), pp.68–77.
2   Credited to Warren Boroson, "What Psychiatrists Say about Goldwater", *Fact*, vol. 1, issue 5 (September/October 1964), p.24.
3   Section 7.3 of the APA's *Principles of Medical Ethics*, p.9.

fact:

VOLUME ONE, ISSUE FIVE $1.25

1,189 Psychiatrists Say Goldwater Is Psychologically Unfit To Be President!

COSMOPOLITAN

JULY 1965

Editor: Helen Gurley Brown

Cover photographer: J Frederick Smith

Cover model: Renata Boeck

Senior editor (from 1968): Jeanette Wagner

Brooke Hauser is the author of *Enter Helen: The Invention of Helen Gurley Brown and the Rise of the Modern Single Woman*, Harper, 2016.

In 1962 Helen Gurley Brown created a publishing phenomenon with her lifestyle guide *Sex and the Single Girl* (Figure 6). With her husband David Brown, an executive at Twentieth Century Fox, she turned it into a franchise, with movie, record, newspaper and TV projects. Editing a woman's magazine was the logical next step. Hearst was looking for "a messiah"[1] to resuscitate its veteran but struggling title *Cosmopolitan*, and offered Helen the job. She became American *Cosmopolitan*'s first female editor since its launch in 1886. She started in March 1965, her first issue was July and it sold out. By December the third-quarter ad revenue was up 50 per cent and circulation was averaging a million copies an issue, almost 15 per cent above 1964.[2]

Two years later Brown summed up her audience: "My kind of swinger is a girl who just wants everything. She may have a career. She does have a love life. She may or may not have children. But she is really living. She is not living through a man, nor does she exploit men. She certainly is not a kept girl – she pays her own bills. She does not go out all night every night and sleep throughout the next day. When she is out late, she arrives at the office sharp at nine the following morning, even though she may be dropping on her feet. She has ideas. This is my credo for *Cosmopolitan* magazine."[3]

BROOKE HAUSER:

That July cover happened by accident. Helen loved the pin-up illustrations J. Frederick Smith had done for *Esquire* and he was assigned to do a story inside *Cosmo*. Most of the models then were kind of flat-chested and slim in the Twiggy mould. But when Helen saw his picture of the blonde busty model Renata Boeck she said, "That's the cover." Renata was German and one of what *Life* magazine had called the "Fraulein Fad"[4] models who were coming to America then. Helen was one of the first female editors to understand that women like to look at other beautiful women.

She was giving a voice to the working girl from a small town, as you can start to see in the cover lines. "When a working girl sees a psychiatrist" is pretty much the quintessential Helen Gurley Brown story. "The new pill" cover line is remembered as being one of the first major magazine stories about birth control. But if you read the article, it's not about what we think of as "the Pill".

JULY, 1965 ● 35¢

COSMOPOLITAN

The new pill that promises to make women more responsive

World's Greatest Lover— What it was like to be wooed by him! From the best-selling book, ALY

When a working girl sees a psychiatrist by Lucy Freeman
PLUS
You Think You're Neurotic by Oscar Levant

The Only Good Secretary— Complete Mystery Novel

Are you a Jax girl? See inside

It's about oestrogen therapy. The story goes that the original line was "the new pill that promises to make women more responsive to men". Hearst objected. Helen was distraught and called David who said, "Take off the last two words – to men." Because what else were they going to be responsive to?

David had been a managing editor at *Cosmopolitan* earlier in his career, and he helped her a lot. Practically every day, certainly for her first few months, she would call him up. He worked nearby, they would get in a cab and drive around Central Park, and she would ask him all of her urgent questions.

JEANETTE WAGNER:

Helen was a visionary. She was very, very focused on her audience which she knew well. She was narrow but deep, I guess I would say. She was not interested in anything particularly political. At one story conference, I suggested that we do an article on one of the women in the Black Panthers. She had no idea who the Black Panthers were. She didn't read *The New York Times* front pages. That was not her mission. Her mission was what she called the mouseburger that she tried to turn into a pussycat. The whole thrust of everything she did was to help that little mouseburger.

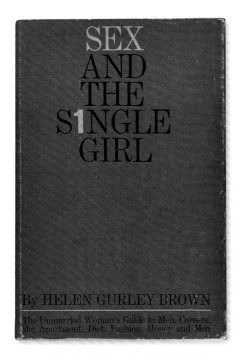

Figure 6 Helen Gurley Brown, *Sex and the Single Girl*, Bernard Geis Associates, 1962.

1 Terry Mansfield interview with Ian Birch.
2 Figures from Chris Welles, "Helen Gurley Brown Turns Editor", *Life*, 19 November 1965, p.66.
3 Quoted in "Helen Gurley Brown talks to Adelle Donen", *Queen* magazine, 10 May 1967.
4 "The Fraulein Fad: German Models are a Big Success in the U.S.", *Life*, 20 March 1964, p.95.

LIFE

25 MARCH 1966

Managing editor: George P Hunt

Los Angeles bureau correspondent:
  Gerald Moore

Cover & feature photographer:
  Lawrence Schiller

Art director: Bernard Quint

Cover credit: Lawrence Schiller –
  Bernard Quint

Launched in 1936, the photography-based news weekly *Life* reached two in five Americans by 1961.[1] One of its long-range assignments was "youth-watching"[2] and that included the rise of LSD. Still legal in 1966, the psychedelic drug was moving from the counterculture to suburbia; it was the perfect moment for the magazine to do a major investigation.

GERALD MOORE:

Larry Schiller had found some young people who were going to drop acid and had agreed to let him photograph them in a West LA apartment. We were there from eight in the evening until the next morning. Once in a while somebody would laugh or talk out loud or cry, but there wasn't a lot of emotion that you could *see*. Later, there was a lot of concern about being able to identify these people. We had their permission but the *Life* lawyers were still worried. It turned out that the young blonde woman in the pictures was the daughter of a General Electric vice-president. She had run away from home and nobody knew where she was.

At the same time that we were doing the LSD story, there was a discussion about a joint venture between Time Inc. and General Electric. The GE vice-president decided that we had identified this girl as his daughter and that we were going to print the photographs as a way of intimidating General Electric in the joint venture process. The lawyers had the art department make minor changes to her face so that a stranger looking at a picture of her and then looking at the pictures in *Life* wouldn't be able to say it was the same person.

Ken Kesey and the Merry Pranksters came to LA to put on an "Acid Test" dance. If there were a hundred people – they were not hippies but pretty conventional – I'd be surprised. It was in a dank old garage. There were two

LIFE

THE EXPLODING THREAT OF THE MIND DRUG THAT GOT OUT OF CONTROL

LSD

TURMOIL IN A CAPSULE

One dose of LSD is enough
to set off a mental riot
of vivid colors and insights
—or of terror and convulsions

MARCH 25 · 1966 ·   35¢

®

garbage cans, one smoking and one not, both filled with Kool-Aid. The one with the dry ice, the smoking one, had been laced with LSD. For a $2 admission fee you could drink as much Kool-Aid as you wanted. Most people drank some and then they basically stood around looking.

The Grateful Dead was supposed to play but something happened to their sound system. So they put recorded music on and had a strobe light. At some point, this guy started dancing and in a dark room with the strobe light going, it was probably the most active thing that happened all evening. I finally realized that these people didn't look like anything was going on but in their heads it was a massive experience.

Everybody convened in New York and agreed it should be a cover. I think Larry said, "Why don't you just put a bunch of LSD pills in somebody's hand and take a picture of it." I'm not sure that's really LSD in my hand. Bernie laid those colour slides on top, I guess, to indicate that there's something more to this than just pills.

We were not happy with that cover slug, "The Exploding Threat of the Mind Drug". It was meant to cover our asses with the social conservatives who were poised to say, "Oh, you're endorsing drugs now." *Life* could say it was reporting on a *threat*. It was a balancing act.

We convinced the editors that we needed to *not* skew the debate so badly that it resulted in the criminalization of LSD. It was criminalized anyway that fall but I don't think we contributed to that. No mainstream magazine had done this kind of comprehensive look at LSD before.

1 Quoted in David E Sumner, *The Magazine Century: American Magazines since 1900*, Peter Lang, 2010, p.90.
2 *Growing Up: The Best of Life*, Time-Life Books, Inc., 1973, p.251.

THE SUNDAY TIMES *magazine*

OCTOBER 24, 1966

Automania

THE SUNDAY TIMES MAGAZINE

24 OCTOBER 1965
24 MARCH 1968
Editor, *The Sunday Times* & editor-in-chief,
    Times Newspapers: Denis Hamilton
    (1959–66)
Magazine editors: Mark Boxer (1962–5)
    & Godfrey Smith (1966–72)
Magazine art director: Michael Rand
Magazine art editor: David King
Magazine writer & film critic: George Perry
Illustrator on *The Sunday Times* newspaper
    and magazine: Roger Law

24 OCTOBER 1965
"Automania" editor: Derek Jewell
Illustrator: Alan Aldridge
Photographer: Denis Rolfe

British newspapers were strictly black and white until 4 February 1962, when *The Sunday Times* introduced a colour section, a 40-page magazine supplement. Heavily criticized at first, it soon added 100,000 sales and created the template for all UK newspaper supplements. Michael Rand's art direction was pivotal, developing "a rather uncomfortable mixture of grit and glamour that gives it tension and contrast".[1] It attracted lucrative new colour advertising and a new wave of brash, classless twenty-something talent; it mixed the high and lowbrow; it drove and defined 1960s culture. "The magazine's philosophy was never to give the public what they want, never to follow taste...No, we should lead taste."[2]

GODFREY SMITH:
I went to my old grammar school in Surbiton to do a talk for the boys. Instead of sitting still, they'd talk to each other and fart and generally be a nuisance. I did my best but, at the end of it, I said, "Look, chaps, what do you like to read about?" One voice said, "Cars." So we invented this word *Automania*, and then Mike started working on this Mini idea.

MICHAEL RAND:
Alan Aldridge, who was a junior in the promotions department at *The Sunday Times*, was also an illustrator. He showed us his portfolio, and we liked it. It reflected the Pop art of that period, so I thought it was a good idea to ask Alan to try a cover. My assistant, David Nathanson, had a Mini, so I dragooned him into lending it to us and, to his horror, getting Alan to paint it. The artwork was split down the middle of the car. One side was sporty with undertones of Bond and Superman, and on the other side was his wife or girlfriend, which reflected home, security and prettiness. Alan whitewashed the car and spent five days doing it. He used a hundred tubes of designers' gouache and six cans of Woolworth's silver spray. We were thrilled about it. Denis Rolfe then photographed it.

   David was somewhat upset by the result. I suggested to David that he keep it because it would become a collector's piece and probably worth a lot of money but, no, he had to have it all washed off. I think he lost an opportunity there.

---

1   Michael Rand interview with Ian Birch.
2   George Perry interview with Ian Birch.

24 MARCH 1968
Photographer: Don McCullin

The cover announces Don McCullin's harrowing 12-page photo essay, "This Is How It Is". He photographed and wrote about the US Marines' bloody counteroffensive to take back the South Vietnamese city of Hue, which the North Vietnamese had captured in the Tet Offensive. The story won the coveted D&AD[1] Silver and Gold Awards in 1969.

MICHAEL RAND:
We decided to start a five-week series on America with this. It's one of his strongest Vietnam essays. Don became a sort of hero to the public at that time. He had an enormous effect on the quality of *The Sunday Times*.

GODFREY SMITH:
We didn't spare anyone's feelings when Don was in action. These pictures weren't news pictures: they were saying, "This is what war is like." Don is a very mild, rather gentle fellow who had this wonderful empathy with soldiers.

MICHAEL RAND:
Don used to shoot in black and white. We didn't impose on him to shoot in colour, but, in the end, he did and, somehow, he shot *harder* in colour. He didn't consciously shoot covers. I mean, he was shooting war. You couldn't actually ask a lot of photographers then to shoot a cover. I don't think many of them understood covers.

ROGER LAW:
It's a terrible thing to say but the adrenaline round the office was unbelievable when McCullin's stuff came in. Michael would discuss the presentation of the pictures with David who did that layout. David was a very important magazine designer at that time. *The Sunday Times* colour magazine was the newest thing since sliced bread and everybody wanted to work on it. Well, we did! David and I were very young and we had a really fucking irresponsible ball. Michael Rand was our mentor.

1 Design & Art Direction Awards – internationally prestigious awards in design and advertising.

NOVA

JANUARY 1966

Editor: Dennis Hackett

Art director & cover photography:
   Harri Peccinotti

Cover star: Sonia Williams, aged four

Art director (1969–75): David Hillman

The *Nova* magic kicked in when Dennis Hackett joined in September 1965, a few months after launch. Harri Peccinotti's radical design and photography perfectly complemented Hackett's equally radical content.

HARRI PECCINOTTI:

It was one of those times when art directors at advertising agencies, like me, suddenly realized that magazines were freer and less restrictive, and were getting more adventurous. We were being impressed by *Town* and *Queen* and *Twen* and Henry Wolf at *Esquire* and *Show* and Herb Lubalin's *Eros*. There was incredible enthusiasm for magazine design.

Racialism in England was really bad in the mid-1960s. Almost still like "No Irish, no blacks, no dogs". There was an article about the problem, so Hackett and I thought of doing a cover. We decided that we would *not* put a sinister picture like a poverty-stricken area on the cover. That would have been the obvious thing to do. Instead, we thought we'd do a little girl like when she goes to church on a Sunday. Hackett wrote the title. I'm not sure I like it but he was very good at one-line titles. He wanted *Nova* to be provocative, that's for sure.

I took the photograph. It was just a little shot in my studio. The girl came with her mum and auntie. They dressed her up: we didn't do anything. We told them what sort of thing we wanted, but we didn't try to engineer it that way. I sometimes cringe a bit about it. Why? I don't know. It makes me uncomfortable probably because I'm one of the people the cover is aiming at. It's like being frightened to face up to what your country does or doesn't do.

CAROLINE BAKER:

Harri was a very political person, very into equal rights for everybody. He was horrified by the treatment of black people. He found black women really beautiful and always photographed them.

HARRI PECCINOTTI:

I don't remember any particularly bad reaction to the cover. I personally detest the idea of market research, asking people in the street what they think. I used to get into rows with Hackett and with those people who said, "What, you don't want to know what people think?" I never, ever paid attention to how many sold or who they sold to.

JANUARY 1966 THREE SHILLINGS

NOVA

YOU MAY THINK I LOOK CUTE
BUT WOULD YOU LIVE NEXT DOOR
TO MY MUMMY AND DADDY?

Start reading on page 14

VOGU

MARCH 1 1966 4/-

COLLECTIONS

VOGUE

MARCH 1966

Editor: Beatrix Miller
Photograph: David Bailey
Cover model: Donyale Luna

Born Peggy Ann Freeman in Detroit in 1945, Donyale Luna became fashion's first internationally celebrated African-American model. Her rise was meteoric: discovered by photographer David McCabe in 1964, she was on the cover of *Harper's Bazaar* by January 1965, though they used a drawing of her with an equivocally pinkish skin tone. In December she decamped to London, and three months later was the first woman of colour on the cover of British *Vogue* – eight years before American *Vogue* made a similar leap. "She happens to be a marvellous shape," editor Bea Miller told *Time*. "All sort of angular and immensely tall and strange. She has a kind of bite and personality."[1]

DAVID BAILEY:

There was a discussion with Bea about who we should use for the cover. There always was. Of course, she didn't give me a brief. I just do what I want. That's why I don't work with a lot of people because I can't do what they want. I'm great friends with Anna Wintour but I don't want to work with her. What she wants is nothing to do with what I do.

Donyale was a beautiful creature. An extraordinary-looking girl. She was a bit nervous. She had those flirty eyes. She was so skinny that she looked taller than she actually was. The hand? I used to do that a lot. It's a thing I got off Picasso who often showed one eye. Some people have said it was to hide she was black. That's the most stupid thing I've ever read.

I didn't care what colour she was. It didn't make a difference to me. We didn't do this thinking this was the first black cover. We did it because she was right for the job. It was at the right moment. There were more pictures of her inside with Moyra Swan and Peggy Moffitt.[2] Alexander Liberman, the creative head of *Vogue*, did say to me if you ever do pictures like that again, you won't work for Condé Nast. I thought it was because the pictures were lesbian-ish but, on reflection, I think it was because Donyale was black. I think he was trying to tell me not to mix pictures like that: this is just something I've thought of recently.

I'm sure *Vogue* got complaints. They got complaints all the time about Jean Shrimpton's legs. I pulled skirts up and sometimes *Vogue* would airbrush them down again. There seemed to be a lot of complaints from Scotland.

1 "Fashion: The Luna Year", *Time*, 1 April 1966.
2 Models Moyra Swan and Peggy Moffitt were both white.

DISC
and MUSIC ECHO 9d

JUNE 11, 1966   USA 25c

MERSEY UPROAR

after 'Whole Scene' attack

SEE PAGE 6

SANDIE
TV miming no CRIME!
Page 7

MERSEYS
jealous of the Hollies!
Page 8

CILLA
I just can't stop myself GIGGLING!
Page 8

BEATLES: WHAT A CARVE-UP!

BEATLES WEEK! They're back with a single, "Paperback Writer" and "Rain"—out tomorrow (Friday).

BUT WHAT'S THIS? The Beatles as butchers, draped with raw meat! Disc and Music Echo's world exclusive colour picture by Bob Whitaker is the most controversial shot ever of John, Paul, George and Ringo.

THE PLACE: A private studio in Chelsea, London. Whitaker is taking some new pictures of the Beatles, and decides that a new approach is needed.

"I wanted to do a real experiment — people will jump to wrong conclusions about it being sick," says Whitaker. "But the whole thing is based on simplicity — linking four very real people with something real.

"I got George to knock some nails into John's head, and took some sausages along to get some other pictures. Dressed them up in white smocks as butchers, and this is the result—the use of the camera as a means of creating situations."

PAUL'S comment after the session: "Very tasty meat."

GEORGE: "We won't come to any more of your sick picture sessions."

JOHN: "Oh, we don't mind doing anything."

RINGO: "We haven't done pictures like THIS before . . ."

Well, what's YOUR verdict? Sick—or super? Six LPs for the best six captions—of no more than 12 words—to the picture above. Send your entry to "Beatles Picture," Disc and Music Echo, 161 Fleet Street, London, E.C.4, before next Friday, June 17.

● PAUL in his own write—exclusive interview: Page 9.

DISC AND MUSIC ECHO

11 JUNE 1966

Editor: Ray Coleman
Photographer: Robert Whitaker

Disc and Music Echo was the first and only British pop music weekly to put an image from a new shoot the Beatles had done in March 1966 with Robert Whitaker on the cover. Whitaker's plan was to create a surreal triptych that sabotaged the popular perception of the Fab Four, but the project was never completed.

"I wanted to do a real experiment – people will jump to wrong conclusions about it being sick," Whitaker says on the front page. Controversy erupted a few days later when a second photograph from the set, with added toy dolls (Figure 7), was revealed as the cover of a new American LP, *The Beatles Yesterday and Today*. "I especially pushed for it to be an album cover,"[1] Lennon later admitted. Capitol Records, their American label, panicked, recalled the LP and then hit on the idea of pasting "a more generally acceptable"[2] photograph over the "Butcher"[3] sleeve. George Harrison thought the session was "gross"[4] and "stupid"[5] while Paul McCartney was more sanguine: "To us, this wasn't a big deal really because these kind of shocking things were part of the art scene"[6]. How the paper got this alternate shot and why it reversed the transparency remains unclear.

ROBERT WHITAKER:[7]

He [the Beatles' then PR, Tony Barrow] hated the session basically because he had six other journalists, all wanting to do interviews, and I was taking a long time. The Beatles were highly amused by what I was up to.

I'd got fed up with taking these Tony Barrow, squeaky-clean pictures of the Beatles, and I thought I'd revolutionize what pop idols are. They were all OK with it right up until the point where I started bringing trays of meat onto the set. Tony Barrow says the dolls were all dismembered. They weren't. They were exactly how I got them, in a box from the manufacturers. I asked for some dolls. I'd gone to Barley Mow Meadows where there was a doll factory, and they said, "Oh, we've only got bits."

They threw them in a box, which I emptied out in front of the Beatles. They then fiddled around with them – George has got an arm on his shoulder, Ringo's got a spare leg. John loved it. I shot them with eyes open, and eyes closed. George, because he was becoming a vegan, wasn't overly impressed. He said he'd never attend another of my photo sessions. I was rather amazed to see that Paul wrote rather favourably about it.[8] Ringo, being the sportsman that he is, I don't think was bothered either way.

According to Tony Barrow, Epstein wanted to burn the transparencies. But I don't know what to believe.

Figure 7 The original, recalled "Butcher" cover of The Beatles Yesterday and Today.

1 Quoted in The Beatles: Eight Days A Week – The Touring Years (dir. Ron Howard), Imagine Entertainment, Apple Corps, 2016.
2 Extracted from the letter to reviewers from Ron Tepper, Manager Press & Information Services, Capital Records Distribution Corp., 14 June 1966.
3 Called "Butcher" because of the white butcher coats and slabs of meat.
4 George Harrison in The Beatles Anthology, Cassell & Co, 2000, p.204.
5 Ibid.
6 Quoted in The Beatles: Eight Days A Week – The Touring Years (dir. Ron Howard), , Imagine Entertainment, Apple Corps, 2016.
7 Extracted from Jon Savage's interview with Robert Whitaker in April 1966, part of which he used for 1966: The Year the Decade Exploded, Faber & Faber, 2015. Reproduced with the author's kind permission.
8 See The Beatles, The Beatles Anthology, Cassell & Co, 2000, p.204.

INTERNATIONAL TIMES

ISSUE 8, 13–26 FEBRUARY 1967

Editor: Tom McGrath

Explosions: John Hopkins

Art editor: Mike McInnerney

Operations: Peter Stansill

Front-page graphics: Mike McInnerney

ISSUE 52, 14–27 MARCH 1969

Editor and words: Peter Stansill

Art editor: Graham Keen

Images/layout: Graham Keen

Cover photography: Horace Ove[1]

The *International Times* (frequently abbreviated to *IT*) was Britain's first underground newspaper. Founded by the core team of John "Hoppy" Hopkins, (Barry) Miles, Jim Haynes and Jack Henry Moore, it was launched at London's Roundhouse on 15 October 1966 with a fund-raising "All Night Rave" which included live performances from Soft Machine and Pink Floyd. The rough-and-ready first issues "focused on avant garde art, music, happenings, theatre, film and literature, with occasional forays into censorship, personal freedom, the Vietnam war, student protests, and LSD and cannabis price trends in Notting Hill".[2]

MIKE MCINNERNEY:

The covers up until then had been mostly type – news items about alternative cultural activities and campaigning issues. I decided to make this one less like a newspaper and more like a periodical. It was my first full issue as art editor. I was trying to signal a kind of a new hippie universe with a counterculture mandala. The arabesque shapes have the symmetry of a mandala which is a balanced geometric composition that usually contains deities. But instead of deities I added the image of an exotically dressed female, a medieval woodcut of a mandrake figure and the *IT* girl[3] which had been established as our logo.

PETER STANSILL:

I became editor in 1968. Graham Keen, the art director, was there and that was it, basically. We had a whole crew of freelancers and it was like herding cats. Everybody was smoking dope and dropping acid. Everything was instant and unconsidered, often ill-considered, but the circulation just soared.

There was still that taboo about black/white interracial relationships. That's what we wanted to break. This might have been a provocative cover but not to us. I never asked anybody outside our readership what they thought about it. It was of no interest to me how it would be accepted, or not, in the wider world. The photograph was by the Trinidadian-British photographer Horace Ove who was documenting the emerging black consciousness in the UK. There are no cover lines. No accompanying story. It was, let's just send a visual message. We didn't need to comment on it. Horace's photograph is perfect.

1 Horace Ove started as a reportage photographer for *IT*, *Oz* and *Race Today* before becoming a distinguished filmmaker: his films include *Baldwin's Nigger* (1969), *Reggae* (1970) and *Pressure* (1975), the first full-length feature by a black director in Britain.

2 Peter Stansill, "The Life and Times of IT", 2016.

3 It was meant to be Clara Bow, the original Hollywood "It Girl", but a picture of Theda Bara was used by mistake.

The International Times   No 8   Feb 13-26 1967/1s

ginsberg • townshend (who) • snyder • mandrake root

it

NO. 52,   MARCH 14-27, 1969   UK 1/6

SQUATTERS START TO RETAKE THE UNIVERSE

(See Centre Spread)

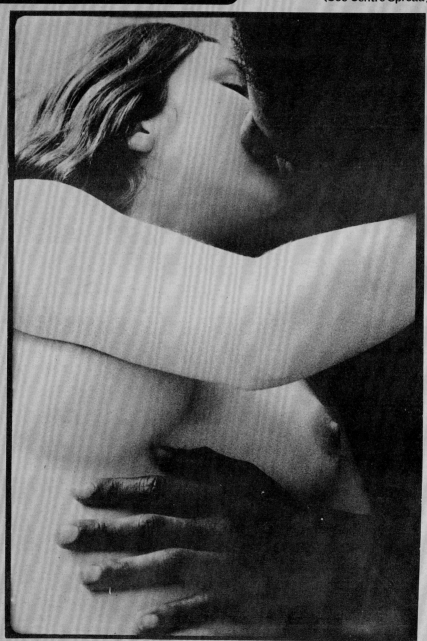

PRINTED AND PUBLISHED BY KNULLAR (PUBLISHING, PRINTING AND PROMOTIONS) LTD., 27. ENDELL ST., LONDON WC2

MANAGEMENT TODAY

FEBRUARY 1968

Editor: Robert Heller

Art director: Roland Schenk

In-house photographer (November 1971 –
February 1972): Brian Griffin

Photographer (February 1968 issue):
Lester Bookbinder

Roland Schenk has been called "a great unsung genius of British magazine design."[1] In the early 1960s he worked at *Du,* the uncompromisingly beautiful Swiss arts and culture magazine which was distributed in 60 countries. This experience was crucial when he became art director of *Management Today* in 1968. Owned by Haymarket Press, it delivered incisive business journalism in a large format and with glossy production values. Notoriously abrasive and demanding, Schenk soon became Haymarket's design director, creating an elegantly robust house style and setting new and exceptional design standards in the British periodical sector. Over the next 30 years he was involved in multiple Haymarket launches, including, notably, *Campaign,* which became the advertising industry's bible.

ROLAND SCHENK:

The ideal cover should transcend the trivial function of content indicator. It should provoke surprise and add an enigmatic dimension, inviting subconscious associations. It should be of artistic quality to prolong its exposure as an object. Cover lines were written later and were of no concern.

This was my first cover for *Management Today.* It satisfies the criteria defined above. The photograph is by Lester Bookbinder. An unusual aspect of the engine was considered. When visiting the Ford factory, Lester discovered this casting block, the mould into which the hot metal is poured, which made for a more surprising image.

BRIAN GRIFFIN:

Lester Bookbinder did the greatest covers that British magazines have ever seen. Incredible abstract still lifes. He is the most unheralded photographer this country has ever had.

ROLAND SCHENK:

I encouraged a non-trivial approach to the subject matter. In the case of *Management Today,* I made it happen due to the harmonious relationship with the editor, Robert Heller. In other cases, I had to resort to terror tactics like cutting short discussions and imposing my decisions in a fierce manner to quell further attempts at argumentation. This was necessitated by operational constraints and is quite contrary to my normal receptive manner.

BRIAN GRIFFIN:

Roland gave me my first break after I left college. I became the photographer for *Management Today* on a retainer of, I think, £25 a week. I began on 1 November 1972 and I left in February 1973, saying, "I'm just not going to work with you any more, I find you too difficult." And he said, "Well, I'm going to continue working with you." He imparted a kind of harsh, antagonistic brutalism which, in fact, shook me up and drove me to find a new way of seeing. It got me to the standard of photography I've now reached.

1   Lindsay Masters quoted in "Haymarket 50 Years: 50 Glorious Moments", *Campaign*, 26 October 2007.

1970s

THE BLACK PANTHER

21 FEBRUARY 1970

Staff: John Seale, Roberta Alexander,
  Brenda Pressley, Mumia Abu-Jamal
  (Wes Cook), Emory Douglas,
  Judi Douglas, Elbert "Big Man" Howard
Cover photography (21 February):
  Stephen Shames

Huey Newton and Bobby Seale formed the Black Panther Party for Self-Defense in October 1966 in Oakland, California, initially as a "civilian police patrol".[1] The following April they launched a weekly newspaper, *The Black Panther: Black Community News Service.*

On 28 October 1967 Newton and a friend were involved in a shoot-out with two officers from the Oakland Police Department. One of the officers, John Frey, was fatally wounded. Newton was arrested for Frey's killing, charged with first-degree murder, and on 8 September 1968 convicted of voluntary manslaughter and sentenced to two to fifteen years in prison. That night, two rogue policemen fired shots at the Panther headquarters, puncturing the iconic poster of Newton hanging in the office window. The following morning, Stephen Shames photographed the mutilated poster, which, sixteen months later, became the cover of a special issue. It was the second edition of *The Black Panther* that week and the sequence of the two covers was telling: the earlier celebrated Newton's 28th birthday on 17 February (Figure 8); the later gave "evidence and intimidation of fascist crimes by U.S.A."[2] In May 1970, Newton's sentence was overturned and a new trial was ordered. By August he was a free man.

THE BLACK PANTHER

25 cents

Black Community News Service

SATURDAY, FEBRUARY 21, 1970   VOL. IV NO. 12

PUBLISHED WEEKLY   **THE BLACK PANTHER PARTY**

MINISTRY OF INFORMATION
BOX 2967, CUSTOM HOUSE
SAN FRANCISCO, CA 94126

SPECIAL EVIDENCE AND INTIMIDATION OF FASCIST CRIMES BY U.S.A. **ISSUE**

THE BLACK PANTHER 25 cents

Black Community News Service

THE BLACK PANTHER PARTY

HAPPY BIRTHDAY HUEY

Figure 8 The Tuesday 17 February cover, released to celebrate Newton's birthday.

STEPHEN SHAMES:

I first came across Bobby at the San Francisco Peace March on April 15, 1967. It was an anti-Vietnam rally. Bobby was selling Mao's *Little Red Book*. I was a student at Berkeley and had a camera, and just out of the corner of my eye, I saw him, slowed down, and snapped one shot. There was a kind of very positive energy coming from him. We became friends and he became my mentor, like a father figure to me.

The Panthers were very, very media conscious. They knew that they needed images, and they liked my photography so we started working together. I saw myself as an artist for the movement. That's how I saw that I could contribute.

The Panthers made alliances with a lot of different groups. There were a lot of white people like me hanging out and working with them. Nowadays, people, especially white people, ask me, "How did you get in with the Panthers?" It's interesting. Black people don't ask that because the black community is open to everyone.

The police were all on alert the day of the verdict. They thought there was going to be a riot and they were ready to go in and kick ass. Bobby kept the Panthers off the streets. He's always been against riots, which he feels are just counterproductive. I mean, it's like a lot of people get killed, businesses get burned, people get arrested, and so what? It doesn't advance anything. Bobby's thing was always to organize, register people to vote, take over. A riot doesn't take over for you. A riot always gets put down. The police have more guns than the rioters.

It was very symbolic when the two police officers blasted that famous poster of Huey. It's like, here's the icon and, boom, they're attacking it. No Panther that I've talked to can remember who took that picture. There are conflicting versions.[3] Bobby says he choreographed the picture. Kathleen Cleaver says that Eldridge, who was her husband, choreographed the picture. At any rate, it was taken at the home of Beverly Axelrod, a white woman who was one of their lawyers and who was also, at that time, Eldridge Cleaver's lover. Someone had the idea to show both Huey's American and African roots. He has a rifle in one hand, a spear in the other and African shields in the background. He's African-American, after all, so why not?

1 Judy Juanita quoted in Lisa Hix, "Black Panther Women: The Unsung Activists Who Fed and Fought for Their Community", *Collectors Weekly*, 2 December 2016.
2 Cover story, 21 February 1970.
3 In its *Art as Activism: Graphic Art from the Merrill C. Berman Collection* exhibition (26 June 2015 – 13 September 2015) the New-York Historical Society states that this photograph is "attributed to Blair Stapp, Composition by Eldridge Cleaver, Huey Newton seated in wicker chair, 1967."

LIFE

15 MAY 1970

Managing editor: Ralph Graves

Cover photography: Howard Ruffner

On 1 May 1970, American and South Vietnamese combat troops crossed into Cambodia. For the anti-war student movement, this extension of the Vietnam War was the last straw. Kent State University in Ohio held demonstrations and the National Guard was sent in. By noon on Monday 4 May, there were approximately 600 National Guardsmen on the campus commons, facing some 2,000 students. The students refused to disperse, the situation degenerated and a group of Guardsmen suddenly opened fire – 67 rounds in 13 seconds. Two men and two women, aged nineteen and twenty, were killed, and nine were wounded.

HOWARD RUFFNER:

I was a photographer for the student-run newspaper *The Daily Kent Stater*. On Monday morning, Bill Armstrong, the editor, received a call from *Life* magazine in Chicago. They were asking if there was anybody who had taken pictures over the weekend. Bill said, "Howard Ruffner, and he's right here." They asked me, "Would you mind covering what happens today?" Hey, it was exciting. I was going to be shooting for *Life*.

I walked down the hill, showed my press pass and crossed over behind the National Guard lines; the media all ended up there. Had I not been working for *Life*, I still question myself, would I have done that or would I have stayed on the side of the students and watched the Guard approach me, as opposed to following the Guard uphill as they approached the students?

LIFE

TRAGEDY AT KENT

Cambodia and Dissent:
The Crisis of
Presidential Leadership

A Kent State student
lies wounded

MAY 15 • 1970 • 50¢

The people who were really protesting were closest to the bottom of the hill. As you went up the hill, I would say 60 or 70 per cent were observers. Kent was a commuter campus and a lot of them had been away for the weekend. There was a mood of confusion and curiosity. What's going on here?

As soon as the last group of Guards reached the highest point, they turned, knelt down in unison and started firing. I thought they would either be shooting blanks or shooting over their heads. I started to hear screaming, "Oh my God, they're shooting real bullets." They were killing people. I took a few pictures of the student who was in front of me. He had been shot a couple of times in the abdomen and he was being attended to by a faculty member. I slowly turned to my left and saw John Cleary, who had also been hit. He was about 115 feet from the National Guard and I started taking pictures of him surrounded by several students attending to him. That's the one that went on the *Life* cover.[1] He was shot in the upper chest but he survived.

I got up and was approached by some students who said, "You gotta stop taking pictures." I said, "I have to take pictures." I was more in shock than scared. You could see the students were stunned, their eyes were glazed over. I felt like I was stealing something from them but I had to do it.

Later, the FBI came to my house: two men in dark suits. They wanted me to identify students in photos and I only told them what they already knew so it wasn't like I was giving them any secrets. But the FBI said, "Now your photographs, Mr Ruffner. Can you share those?" I said, "They're with *Life* magazine. I don't have anything to share with you." As they left, they said, "Well, if that's what you want to do with your blood money, Mr Ruffner..."

The pictures show the truth. I really believe that. I'm trying to get Kent State to put up a mural of all the photographs in as much chronological order as they can because it will show the truth.

1   Most of the photographs for the cover story inside were by three Kent State students: Ruffner, John Filo and John Darnell.

OZ

MAY 1970

Editor: Jim Anderson

Cover credit: "This issue of OZ appears with the help of Jim Anderson, Gary Brayley, Felix Dennis, Bridget Murphy, Richard Neville, Liz Watson and David Wills."

The "school kids" included: Charles Shaar Murray, Peter Popham, Deyan Sudjic, Colin Thomas

Secretary: Marsha Rowe[1]

In 1970 *Oz* co-founder Richard Neville, about to hit 30, felt "old and boring" and invited readers under 18 to edit an issue. This became the infamous "*Oz* School Kids Issue". After the Obscene Publications Squad raided the *Oz* office, Neville and co-editors Jim Anderson and Felix Dennis were charged on two counts: obscenity and conspiracy to corrupt public morals. The trial began on 22 June 1971. The "*Oz* Three" were found not guilty on the conspiracy charge but guilty of two lesser offences. When the case went to appeal, the convictions were quashed.

JIM ANDERSON:

Richard had gone off to Ibiza and left me and Felix in charge. A fantastic set of kids had turned up. We looked at their material, and oh, my goodness, some of the cartoon illustrations ... there was the masturbating headmaster and particularly Vivian Berger's Rupert Bear collage.[2] Brilliant idea, just right for *Oz*.

Peter Ledeboer[3] had come back from Holland with this book *Dessins Erotiques* by the artist Bertrand.[4] It consisted entirely of drawings of this fantasy black woman in a series of erotic poses. There was only one which we and the kids all liked and I marked it for the centre spread. On the very last night, when the kids had all gone home, Felix insisted he wanted the centre spread for his Back Issue Bonanza. Our intended cover of the *Oz* secretary as a St Trinian's schoolgirl running bare-breasted through a playground with an Uzi was not working. That's when I had my fateful idea. "Oh, let's put the naked black ladies on the cover." It fitted perfectly across the front and the back. Felix and I scarcely looked at it because we were busy laying out the pages.

Then, at about two o'clock in the morning, we took a closer look. We were stoned. We were tired. We had to get the thing to the printer by eight. Felix said, "Hmm. We won't get away with the blow job." One woman was giving another a blow job. I had the idea of putting a photograph of one of the schoolboys, the one with the longest hair, over it. Problem solved. We didn't even notice the rat tail coming out of a vagina.

The shit soon hit the fan. We were busted within days and charged with publishing obscene material. Richard had been busted twice before in Sydney for the same thing and only been fined, so we decided not to take it too seriously.

That was it for a while. Then Mr Wilson got defeated in the election and Edward Heath came in. The new Conservative government took another look at

Oz, raised the stakes and dragged up this old common law conspiracy charge – to debauch and corrupt the morals of children and young persons within the Realm and to implant in their minds lustful and perverted desires. They assumed we had coerced the school kids into putting in the sexual material, that we had corrupted them. They saw this as a chance to deal the underground press a mortal blow.

Suddenly, it was all very serious. There were many signals that the 1960s were over, and one of them was the *Oz* trial.

DEYAN SUDJIC:[5]

1970 was my last year at school. It was in West London and very political so there was a hardcore of teenage Maoists. There were three of us: Peter Popham, who went on to become a foreign correspondent for the *Independent*, Colin Thomas, who is a photographer, and me. We saw the ad in *Oz* saying come and tell us what you would do with a school kids issue.

We thought, "that sounds interesting", so we applied. Richard Neville wrote back to say come and talk. We went along under the impression that we would be left to our own devices to do the magazine, and found ourselves in a Holland Park basement with a room of other young and ambitious careerists. It was a very masculine group that included Charles Shaar Murray and Viv Berger but not a lot of women.

It quickly became apparent that School Kids *Oz* was not so much about young people editing a magazine as the theme for an issue that was shaped by Richard, Felix and Jim. The cover came as a complete, and pretty unpleasant, surprise. None of us saw it before the issue came out on the newsstands. The response from my friends made me really understand for the first time that there was such a thing as feminism, and that it mattered.

MARSHA ROWE:

It's an appalling cover. I don't know what Jim and Felix were even thinking of. I mean, we had been for sexual freedom but then it became so that the only view of sexuality was through men's eyes. It was more and more objectifying. But, at that time, I didn't have that sort of analysis. I just thought, "Oh, men and their fantasies", really.

1 Rowe re-joined *Oz* after this issue, worked on their trial defence and later co-founded *Spare Rib* (see page 79).
2 Fifteen-year-old Vivian Berger did a cartoon strip inside which grafted a priapic Rupert Bear onto a story of sexual hijinks by Robert Crumb.
3 Ledeboer had recently quit *Oz*, where he was business manager, to start Big O Posters.
4 Bertrand (illustrator), *Dessins Erotiques*, Eric Losfield, 1969.
5 Deyan Sudjic is currently director of the Design Museum, London.

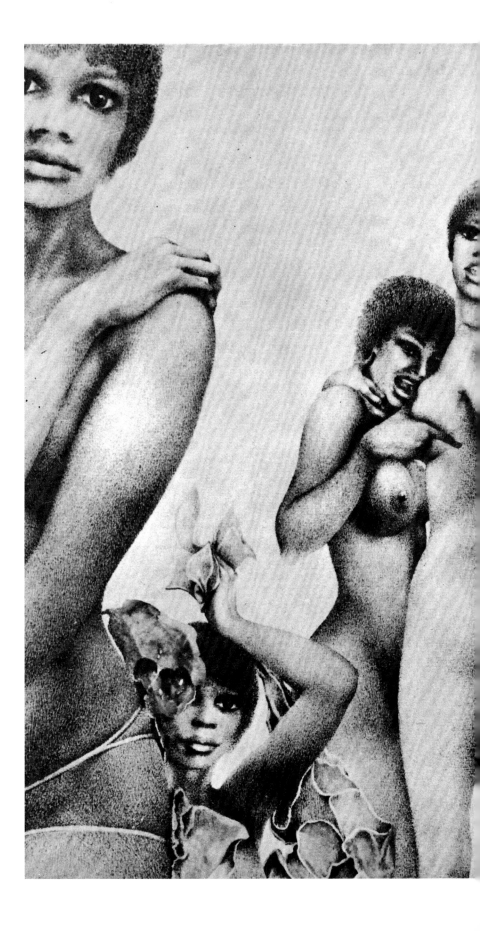

NOVA

SEPTEMBER 1971

Editor: Gillian Cooke
Art director: David Hillman
Fashion editor: Caroline Baker
Cover photography: Hans Feurer
Cap: 50p at Badges & Equipment

Nova's cover for its September 1971 issue has been credited with the invention of street style.

CAROLINE BAKER:

When I arrived at *Nova* in 1965 I was a little mouse who loved fashion and would run around looking like Twiggy. Then I met these really strong personalities like Harri Peccinotti and Hans Feurer who were very into women's lib and was influenced very much by them. *Nova* made me as revolutionary as *Nova* was, I think I could say.

Molly Parkin, the fashion editor, and Dennis Hackett had a major row – she and Dennis always used to row – and Molly left in 1967. Dennis called me in and said, "You look like you are interested in fashion. Do you want to give it a go?" I was like, "Oh, wow." So I became fashion editor. I had done no fashion at all and was suddenly thrown in the deep end. Dennis knew nothing about fashion, but he wanted me to be irreverent.

I had an obsession with dressing girls as boys. I thought men's clothing was so much more comfortable. It was shocking because in those days you didn't do that. In a way, it was what we were all wearing, the uniform of everybody who went on marches. Everybody would be wearing a flak jacket. The American army surplus was wonderful. It was such good cotton compared to the English, and a lot of it came from Laurence Corner.[1] Then it crept into woman's fashion. You could buy it for a few shillings, and be dead cool. This is when "street style" began to establish itself and a lot of fashion fanatics started following my work.

I did this story with Hans Feurer in Corsica. Photographers then were like artists in a way. Because it wasn't so commercial, you had total freedom to

NOVA

SEPTEMBER 1971

20p

ONE MAN'S MEAT IS
ANOTHER MAN'S
GLUCONO-D-LACTONE
DRESSED TO KILL
PETER WALKER:
CABINET SUPERSTAR
FIND THE
FACE THAT FITS YOU
MISSIONARIES
IN THE MELTING POT

interpret ideas that you had. The favourite models then were all Swedish, Dutch, Norwegian and German, who were quite free in their attitude. Those were the days before AIDS when you tended to have affairs with everybody. The pecking order was the photographer first, then the editors and assistants would shack up with the driver. Somehow, it wasn't dangerous. And we weren't settling down, were we, and having kids?

The cover is a close-up of the German model, Christiana, who was a very cool modern girl. I think the story was shocking in two ways: one, it portrayed war as a beautiful, fashionable subject, and, two, it showed women as these tough warriors. *M*A*S*H* was hugely popular at the time, and there was this famous nurse[2] in it. It was very linked to the women's movement and the way women were seeing themselves: "Why can't I be like a man, why can't I do this?"

I never realized how all these people like Calvin Klein and Kenzo were religiously buying *Nova* and would be inspired by what they saw in the magazine, and, a year later, you'd see it on the catwalk. Was I flattered? I was just really surprised.

1 Laurence Corner, at 62 Hampstead Road, London NW1, sold army and navy surplus clothes and accessories very inexpensively. A pair of camouflage trousers used in the shoot cost 63p.
2 Major Margaret J "Hot Lips" Houlihan (played by Loretta Swit).

SPARE RIB

LAUNCH ISSUE, JULY 1972

Editorial: Marsha Rowe and Rosie Boycott
Design: Kate Hepburn and Sally Doust
Cover photography: Angela Phillips

In November 1971 Marsha Rowe, who was working at *Oz* and its short-lived sister publication, *Ink*, invited all the women at *International Times*, *Time Out*, *Friends* and *Oz* to a meeting to discuss their lives in the underground press. It led to a second one in January 1972, when Rowe met Rosie Boycott, then at *Friends*, and suggested starting a magazine. *Spare Rib* launched six months later.

ROSIE BOYCOTT:

Those meetings were unbelievably exciting and completely revolutionary. Women would talk about sex, their mothers, their ambitions, about how they felt stifled by the work they did. What emerged so strongly was that, even though we all worked in "the underground", we were living absolutely traditional lives. We were still the typists, the tea-makers. There were no women editors of any underground papers.

MARSHA ROWE:

It changed lives, that meeting. It's so hard to describe how totally it was a man's world then. A man had to sign if you wanted to hire a television, buy a car or get a mortgage.

ROSIE BOYCOTT:

The underground was an incredibly good place for blokes because they got to take drugs, stay up all night, and, if women didn't want to sleep with them, they could say you're square. It was a very double-edged sword because if you didn't want to be promiscuous, you were a "straight".

MARSHA ROWE:

I thought of a magazine as your friend, your other intimate voice. We aimed to raise £7,000 but only managed £2,000 so we started with a minimal budget. I thought, "Well, obviously it's going to have all the things that a normal women's magazine would have but subverted." Instead of the women's page in the *Guardian*, we had a man's page.

ROSIE BOYCOTT:

Our fiction was by Margaret Drabble, Fay Weldon and Edna O'Brien, so it was amazing. George Best, of course, did not write that man's page – someone else wrote it for him. I don't think it was very good but we were smart enough to see this was a good cover line, and a huge surprise.

Our plan was absolutely not to do an underground magazine. In my head, I thought we could take over from *Woman* and *Woman's Own,* which between them sold about three-and-a-half to four million copies a week. The covers weren't fashion shots, they were more like Oxo Katie[1] shots. The faces on our first cover were something different – un-made up, youthful, friendly, energetic, and two women together. It was about sisterhood. The logo was done by Kate Hepburn who did a lot for Monty Python. Kate was a genius.

MARSHA ROWE:

I wanted a name like *Oz* which was meaningless but meaning could attach to it. I was in a relationship with Andrew Cockburn, the middle son of [the journalist] Claud Cockburn. One night we all went to a Chinese restaurant and Claud came out with this joke about spare ribs.

ROSIE BOYCOTT:

I mean, it's so corny but he picked up a spare rib and said, "That would be a very good title for your magazine." Both of us just said, "Of course." And then it could never be anything else.

ANGELA PHILLIPS:

Almost immediately, *Spare Rib* became controversial within the women's movement for being too traditional. Some of the more purist of the sisters felt that it was a bit of a sell-out. Not alternative enough. But I think that was its strength.

---

1 Long-running British TV commercial for Oxo gravy which started in 1958 and came to represent "Middle England".

spare **Rib**

the new women's magazine
JULY 17½p

The days Women
rocked the World
Georgie Best on Sex
Does the Government
care about Pensioners?
Richard Neville
on the Glossies
Growing up in the
Bosom Boom
8 page News Section
and lots more inside.

INTERVIEW

JULY 1972

Editors: Andy Warhol, Paul Morrissey,
   Fred Hughes
Managing editor & art director:
   Glenn O'Brien
Cover design: Richard Bernstein
Special contributing editor:
   Robert Colacello
Cover photo: Berry Berenson
Cover model: Pat Cleveland

In May 1972 Glenn O'Brien unveiled a new look for the monthly magazine *Interview*. The cover was in full colour for the first time with a bigger, "handwritten" logo that now included Warhol's name, following demands from its new financial backers.[1] This was primarily the work of artist Richard Bernstein and it remained the basic template for the next 15 years. "The overall effect was of an Andy Warhol portrait autographed by Andy Warhol – though Andy's hand had never touched the page," Bob Colacello later wrote.[2] Warhol confirmed this: "Sometimes people think I do the cover of *Interview*. Well, I don't. I haven't the time. But Richard Bernstein's faces are wonderful. They're so colorful and he makes everyone look so famous."[3]

July featured supermodel Pat Cleveland in rapture to a Sony TC-50 cassette recorder and microphone – a piece of technology that Warhol would often introduce to his interviewees as "My wife, Sony". *Interview* would become the insider handbook of "the disco decade".

PAT CLEVELAND:
Richard and Berry were kind of an item at the time. He always wore silk shirts, was very well dressed and had a soft heart. If Richard were a Disney character, he'd be Jiminy Cricket.

Berry was just beginning as a photographer, so Richard gave Berry her first cover job with *Interview*. Berry was the sister of Marisa Berenson, the actress and model, and they were the grandchildren of Schiaparelli. So I was photographed by the granddaughter of Schiaparelli![4] The cover is just the photograph. Richard didn't airbrush me.[5]

We had all been in Fire Island for the weekend and came back into the city in a limo to Berry's loft. She had this beautiful loft painted completely white – white walls, white floors – with lots of light. It was one of those shotgun, straight-through lofts on 2nd Avenue and 57th. At the time, only artists lived in those old buildings.

They transformed it into a studio. It was very amateurish. Berry had her Nikon and Richard guided her on how to get the composition right and set up the strobe lights. They decided to put some technology into the picture. Everybody had to have one of those Sony tape recorders then: it was like the first Walkman.[6] The microphone was a symbol of stardom. Everybody wants to have the mike. Everybody wants to speak into it.

This was the bright and brimming springtime of New York. It would be like if you were in Paris in the 1920s and were hanging out in the Café de Flore[7] where all the writers went. *Interview* was our answer to that.

1 Peter Brant and Joe Allen, sourced from Bob Colacello, *Holy Terror: Andy Warhol Close Up, An Insider's Portrait*, HarperCollins, 1990, p.106.

2 Ibid.

3 Andy Warhol quoted in *Richard Bernstein, Megastar*, Indigo Books, 1984, p.2.

4 Lauded Italian fashion designer at the height of her success between the two World Wars.

5 Bernstein often used collage and airbrush techniques to transform photographs into richly stylized portraits.

6 The first Sony Walkman went on sale on 1 July 1979.

7 Art Deco coffee house favoured by French writers and philosophers in the 1920s.

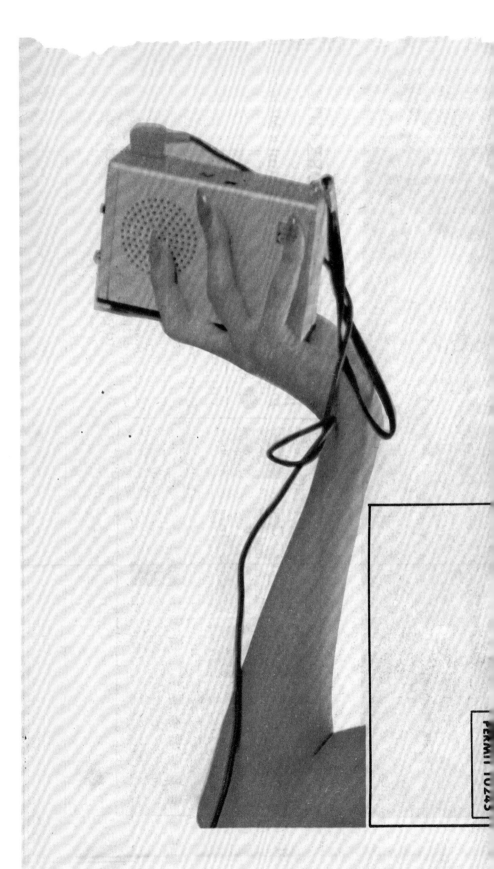

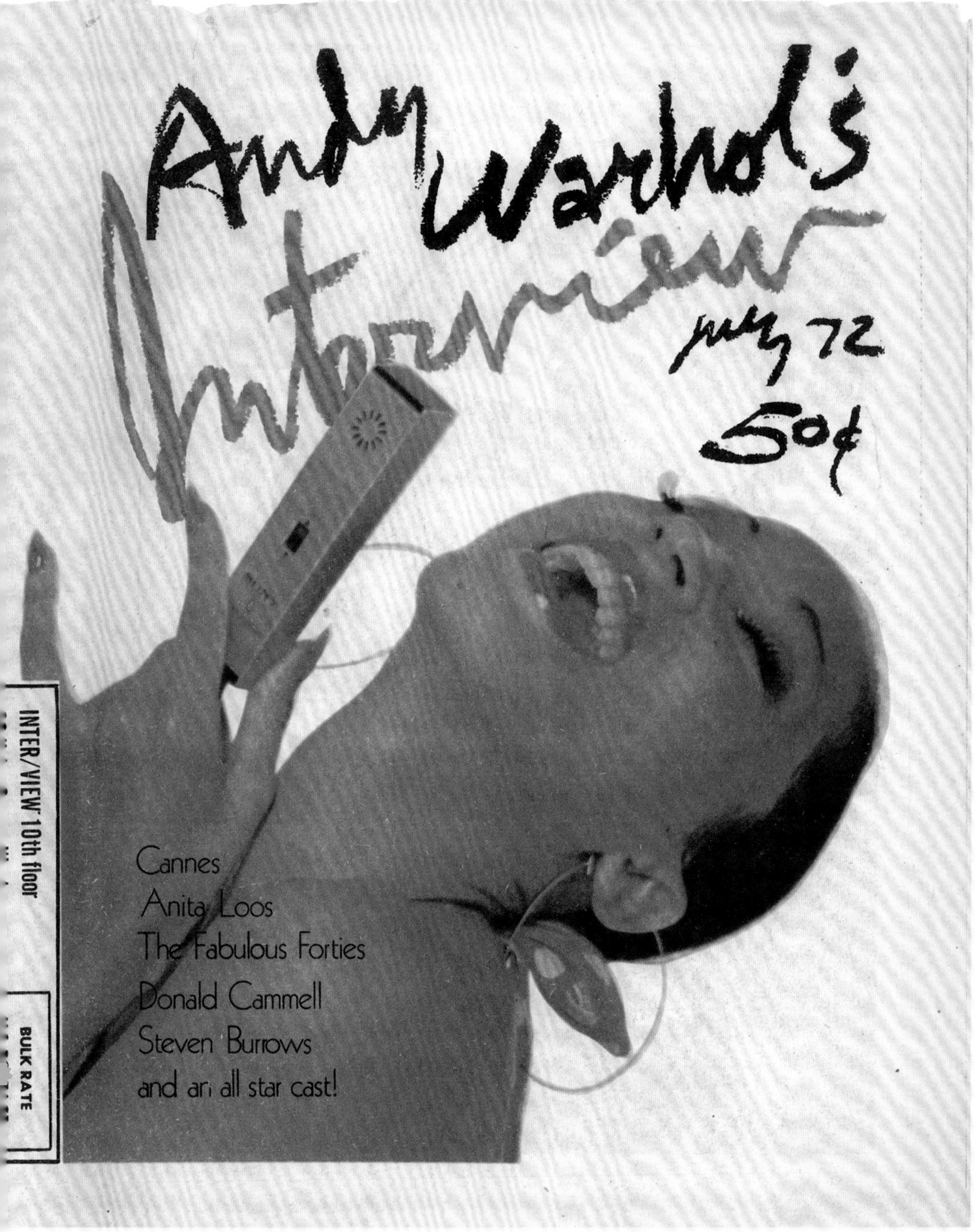

Andy Warhol's Interview

july 72
50¢

INTER/VIEW 10th floor

BULK RATE

Cannes
Anita Loos
The Fabulous Forties
Donald Cammell
Steven Burrows
and an all star cast!

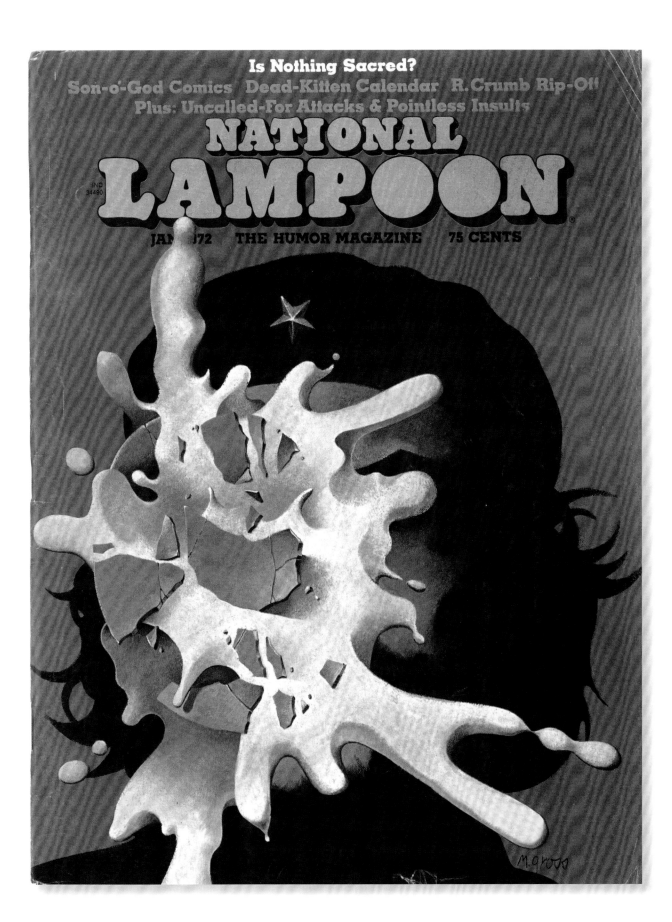

NATIONAL LAMPOON

JANUARY 1972
JANUARY 1973
Managing editor: Tony Hendra
Art director: Michael Gross
Contributing editor: Ed Bluestone
Cover photography: Ronald G Harris

In the early 1970s *National Lampoon*, the satirical monthly created by Harvard graduates Henry Beard, Doug Kenney and Rob Hoffman, was the incarnation of hip for its predominantly campus-based readership. Its notorious January 1973 cover began as a proposed subscription campaign: "If you don't subscribe, we'll kill this dog and, if that doesn't work, a cat, and the animal death toll will rise until you do." The campaign did not run but it was the perfect cover for the death-themed issue. "The shot was extremely hard to get; when the dog looked straight out at the reader he simply appeared victimized. Then someone had the notion of actually pulling the trigger. The dog reacted to the noise and this was the result."[1]

Without *National Lampoon*, there probably would not have been *Saturday Night Live*. It incubated talents like John Belushi, Bill Murray, Chevy Chase and Gilda Radner. British-born Tony Hendra was there from the start. He had come from the comedy duo Hendra and Ullett, regular performers on American TV variety shows in the 1960s.

TONY HENDRA:

The level of censorship on American television in the 1960s was acute. It basically meant that people of my generation could not mention or discuss any of the things that were on our minds, whether it was the sexual revolution, or liberation of any kind, and certainly not the Vietnam War. So it was a source of explosive frustration. Going to the *Lampoon* was like walking out of a dark room into sunlight.

The Che cover with the cream pie was my first issue as managing editor, which was kind of a ridiculous term because there was no way to keep that bunch in any kind of management whatever.

I insisted that the title of the issue be "Is Nothing Sacred?" because that seemed to me to be a kind of modish, postmodern way of self-referencing, and so seemed to poke fun both at the people who were outraged and its actual target. I think it was me who said, "I don't think there's anything more sacred on campus at the moment than the Paul Davis Che poster." Everyone went, "Yeah, I guess so, and we fucking hate it." Nobody hated Paul Davis, but they thought the sanctification of that particular image was really obnoxious. I had originally wanted to take the poster and slam a cream pie onto it but Gross decided he wanted to show off his art skills, and do a parody of Paul Davis because he was an Ayn Rand fan. He did a lovely job.

The dog cover was Ed's idea. He was a wonderfully irreverent comedian who had a real hang-up about death. Casting was obviously crucial and the dog we eventually got was modelled on Freckles, my very sweet mutt who had a big patch on one eye. In a funny way, it was more moderate than a lot of the other covers we did around that period but it did nail the fact that what is really sacred for every American family is pets. So that was what gave it, if you'll excuse the expression, legs. Were people outraged by it? Absolutely. We certainly couldn't do that cover today without being shot, or banned for ever.

---

1 Tony Hendra, *Going Too Far*, Dolphin Doubleday, 1987, pp.244–5.

Death
The Adventures of Deadman Playdead Magazine
Last-Aid Kit Suicide Letters to Santa

NATIONAL
LAMPOON

IND
34490

JAN. 1973, THE HUMOR MAGAZINE 75 CENTS

If You Don't Buy This Magazine, We'll Kill This Dog

Time Ou

London's
Living Guide
October 12-18 1973 No.190 15p

Jealousy

You're liberated.
You're hip.
You don't mind.
Do you?

TIME OUT

12–18 OCTOBER 1973
25 NOVEMBER–1 DECEMBER 1977
5–11 MAY 1978
Publisher/sometime editor: Tony Elliott
Art director/cover design:
    Pearce Marchbank

Pearce Marchbank became art director of the pocket-sized fortnightly *Time Out* in early 1971. He introduced a radically new information architecture, lobbied to increase the format to the bigger A4 and make it a weekly, both of which happened with the 29 April 1971 issue. He soon left, but continued designing most of the covers on a consultancy basis until 1983. Lean, clean and witty, these set a benchmark in the evolution of the counterculture press through the 1970s.

PEARCE MARCHBANK:

I always assumed no one wants to buy the magazine so they've got to be given a kick up the bum to buy it. That's what I tried to do.

I redesigned the logo. I wasn't that pleased with it but the reaction was good, so we kept it. To tell you the truth, I didn't like the letter "T". It's a weak letter. There are very few swear words that start with a T and it hasn't got a flat left-hand side which is a pain for lining things up. The idea was that the logo was out of focus like a neon sign, which suggested entertainment, obviously, but it was transparent. The logo could be obliterated or partly readable or hover like a mark on a windowpane over the image. It gave you immense freedom.

I did win a fantastic battle with the money people in *Time Out* about the "Jealousy" cover because it sold out immediately. They said it was the worst cover they'd ever had but that shut them up. It was a very abstract piece about sexual jealousy: hence green with envy. It was before the days when people thought you had to put the contents of the magazine on the cover. *Cosmopolitan* was the start of the rot. Just have one thing on the cover and, if you really did have a special, put a flash in the corner.

There were open auditions for the *Elvis* musical at the Astoria Theatre in the West End, so anyone could go down and present themselves. I thought, would you get the part if you looked just like him? Let's do an Elvis mask you could stick on your face. It was nearly life-size. Unfortunately, Richard Williams, the editor at the time, changed the cover line. I wanted, "Put on the mask and go to the theatre at ten o'clock next Tuesday", or words to that effect. Richard changed it to "In the future, everybody will be Elvis for 15 minutes", a twist on the Andy Warhol saying, which doesn't have anything to do with the auditions.

My jokey ethos was the nearer to the Japanese flag you can get, the better the cover. The "red football" cover is the nearest I got. I remember we had nothing to go with. There were two football finals in one week,[1] so I asked Richard Williams if there was any combining factor about the teams, Arsenal and Liverpool. He said, "Yes, they're both red." I got a football sprayed red and stuck it on the cover. which was not really anything to do with anything but it led you into the piece.

TONY ELLIOTT:

The cover I always quote as being a classic is the "red football". We took it to a car spray place and had it sprayed Liverpool red. It's just so beautifully executed.

In the future, everybody will be Elvis for 15 minutes.

London's Living Guide
Nov 25-Dec 1 1977 No. 399 30p

Jack Good is making dreams come true for P.J. Proby, Shakin' Stevens, and Timothy Whitnall. Cut-out the mask, turn to page 12 and join the club.

---

1 Arsenal v Ipswich, FA Cup (6 May) and Liverpool v Bruges, European Cup (10 May).

Time Out

May 5-11 1978 No.422 30p

Red is the colour.

Clough's Forest having nicked Div. One and the League Cup, can Arsenal and Liverpool make it a red flush in this week's FA and European cup finals? Inside, we talk to the men who make them tick.

NEW MUSICAL EXPRESS

19 JANUARY 1974

Editor: Nick Logan
Assistant editor: Ian MacDonald
Cover photography: Pennie Smith
Features: Charles Shaar Murray, Nick Kent

In early 1972 the new editor, Alan Smith, and his deputy, Nick Logan, were given 12 weeks to save a floundering *New Musical Express.* They did it in part by raiding the underground press for a younger, hipper editorial team, including Charles Shaar Murray, Nick Kent, Ian MacDonald and Pennie Smith. Sales soared from around 60,000 to 200,000 by the end of 1973, when Smith left and Logan, then 26, took over. He was faced almost immediately with a printers' strike in November, which kept the paper off the streets for nine weeks. This first post-strike issue introduced Logan's vision, which would turn the paper into Britain's most influential music weekly.

NICK KENT:

The strike was a very nervous time. We'd suddenly become really successful and then, boom, it was like an amputation for nine weeks. But Nick was able to plot.

NICK LOGAN:

I love this cover. In my opinion, it was the beginning of *NME*'s golden period. That's what makes it revolutionary, important.

I think it was the first time I introduced a full-page image on the front. I love the confidence and the Monty Python style of humour: taking the piss, basically. That wouldn't have happened without the strike, when there was also an enormous amount of bonding in the office. The issue looked so good and had such good content. It did feel like you'd released a dam of pent-up energy. Actually, at that time I thought, "This is going to be a hell of a ride." I wasn't sure

NEW

MUSICAL EXPRESS

January 19, 1974   U.S. 50c/Canada 35c   8p

HELLO HELLO

WE'RE BACK AGAIN

EMERGENCY 3-DAY
CANDLELIGHT CRISIS
SHOCK SCANDAL ISSUE

**Jethro/Mott/Lennon
Sayer/Santana/ELP**

BYRON FERRARI: PRINCE OF SLEAZE

PAGE 18

Pic: PENNIE SMITH

what I was unleashing, and I thought, "Someone will get damaged here", and they did, and it was me[1] – and other people, of course.

PENNIE SMITH:

Nick left everybody to do what they enjoyed doing so he got the best from them. The photos were as important as the copy and they weren't cropped. I appreciated that because I shoot full frame, so luckily the front of the *NME* is more or less a 35mm frame. It was straight art, for want of a better word.

I think my advantage is that I didn't get involved with the music business, so I had a clean brain every time I did a shoot. I was interested in people and I shot them like they were my auntie. I have worked my whole life through innocence and in that way it's inadvertently come over as left field.

I had done some Roxy Music stuff before this. There was just Bryan, his PR chap, Dr Simon Puxley, and me walking along the beach at Bournemouth. Bryan was incredibly camera shy and I remember making a couple of rude jokes which made him laugh. Everything worked out a treat.

NICK KENT:

It was a great photograph. We were all works-in-progress as writers and photographers and the first fruition for many of us was that issue. You have to remember how fast things went then. Marc Bolan was a has-been at this point. David Bowie was still top dog but he was focused on America. That meant Roxy Music owned the British Isles. It was their fiefdom. Nick also viewed Ferry very highly.

PENNIE SMITH:

The cover looked like something new. It definitely felt classy and I don't think it's really dated. The *NME* was on such tosh paper, like orange wrapper paper, that I always printed my photos really hard so they looked very graphic on the page. Byron Ferrari? That used to get up Ferry's nose. He was referred to as something different every time[2] but I think it was done with affection.

---

1   Logan had a nervous breakdown in late 1976.
2   Ferry "misspellings" included Brain Fury, Biryani Ferret and Brawn Fairy.

PEOPLE WEEKLY

LAUNCH ISSUE, 14 MARCH 1974
Managing editor: Richard B ("Dick") Stolley
Cover photography: Steve Schapiro

People's mantra was ordinary people doing extraordinary things and extraordinary people doing ordinary things. Dick Stolley masterminded a mix of human interest stories that were told in a zesty, empathetic and scrupulously fact-checked way, and which he labelled "personality journalism" to separate it from pure "celebrity journalism". Parent company Time Inc. had poured an estimated $40 million into the launch and, astonishingly, within only 18 months it was making money and went on to become Time Inc.'s most profitable magazine – and a national institution. "This was the beginning of the 'Me Decade'," Stolley later said. "We found out that people in the news were quite willing to talk to us about themselves. They'd talk about a lot of personal things – their sex lives, their money, their families, religion. They'd talk about things that a few years earlier wouldn't even have been brought up."[1] He wrote "Stolley's Law of Covers",[2] which *People* still references today.

DICK STOLLEY:
I wince every time I look at that launch cover. We made several mistakes. First of all, no eye contact. And the timing was bad. The movie didn't open for three weeks.[3] We had too many cover lines down the side and they were all the same type size. We should have had two or three in large type and maybe one or two in small. The mistakes that we made were so monumental that it is a great tribute to the idea that it was good enough to overcome all of these blunders.

We decided that this would be a newsstand magazine. Time Inc. had not had a newsstand magazine since 1936 when *Life* started. Now, Time Inc. had no distribution system but we decided that we would promise a million sales every week. You just wonder what the hell was the thinking. That first issue, with all the publicity, sold nearly a million,[4] which was extraordinary, and then it went back down to about a half a million. After a few weeks it became apparent to our publisher, Richard J Durrell, a very smart guy, that we were going to have to spend a few million dollars to set up our own newsstand distribution system, which we did. Within a few weeks it worked.

The dumbest thing I did while editing *People* was not to put Elvis on the cover when he died. Time Inc. back then had a policy of never putting dead people on the cover. I should have been smart enough to ignore that strange tradition; I spent a weekend with Elvis once and I liked him, but he had gotten fat and sweaty, with smaller and smaller audiences, and I guess that's what convinced me. Anyway, I made the decision, nobody argued with me, and then, after we closed the magazine,[5] I went around to thank everybody because it was very late, two or three o'clock in the morning. They had radios turned on to Elvis songs and some were even crying. I thought, "Jesus Christ, did I screw up on this one?" To compensate, I put him on the cover five times in the next year. I quickly discovered that dead celebrities were among our bestselling covers, and still are.

1 Quoted in Curtis Prendergast (with Geoffrey Colvin), *The World of Time Inc.*, Atheneum, 1986, p.440.
2 Stolley's Law of Covers: "Young is better than old. / Pretty is better than ugly. / Rich is better than poor. / Television is better than movies. / Movies are better than music. / Music is better than sports. / Anything is better than politics. / And nothing is better than the celebrity dead."
3 *The Great Gatsby* (dir. Jack Clayton) was released 27 March 1974.
4 The launch issue sold very close to the target million – 978,000.
5 The cover, dated 29 August 1977, featured Ann-Margret and Marty Feldman. Elvis's death was covered by a 27-line item on the "Star Tracks" page.

14227

People
weekly

March 4, 1974   35 Cents

Mia Farrow
In 'Gatsby,'
the year's next
big movie

VOGUE

AUGUST 1974

Editor-in-chief: Grace Mirabella
Model: Beverly Johnson
Photographer: Francesco Scavullo
Fashion editor: Frances Stein

This was American *Vogue*'s first cover with a model of colour. It was so successful that Johnson was given a second the following June. *The New York Times* weighed the significance: "If, as some sociologists believe, fashion reflects social change, Beverly on the cover of *Vogue* is announcing that racial strife is in a cooling off period, that the Panthers have gone establishment in Oakland, and that the Black Muslims have deleted the expression 'white devil' from their vocabulary and are recruiting white members."[1] Grace Mirabella had a different take. In the same article she said, "We don't think of it as a milestone but I'm very proud to have had her there."

BEVERLY JOHNSON:

I had been working since 1971 and had done many covers of magazines like *Glamour*. But I now set my focus on *Vogue*. When I told my agent, Eileen Ford, that's what I wanted, she said, "Forget about it. You'll never be on the cover." I thought there is no reason to ask why. I knew she would never change her position. That's when I knew I had to leave the Ford Modeling Agency. So I left her – very nicely – and went to the Wilhelmina Agency, run by the Dutch model Wilhelmina Cooper. She said, "I can do it", and she did.

I didn't know it was going to be a cover: it was just a regular shoot. When it came out, the calls started. The first one was from Kenya. They asked me, "How does it feel to be the first woman of colour on *Vogue*?" I said, "What are you talking about? That's impossible. This is the Seventies. Didn't we do all the civil rights in the Sixties?"

In 1974 *Vogue*'s circulation tripled and they didn't attribute that to the fact that now black women were buying it. That's how in denial they were. Grace knew – everyone knew – but it was a secret they didn't want people to know.

What was interesting was the reaction from other models. I knew black models were always jealous, which I understood because I was the "token", right? But I wasn't prepared for the white models. I always worked on a white set – everyone was white apart from me – and they snubbed me. It was like, you can be on the cover of *Glamour* and all those other magazines, but not *Vogue*. Now, you've crossed the line. You're top in the coloured water fountain over there, but you can't be top of the white water fountain over here. I couldn't claim what I had accomplished. So it really was an awakening for me. I call myself the Jackie Robinson of the fashion industry.[2]

---

1   Ted Morgan, "I'm the biggest model, period", *The New York Times*, 17 August 1975.
2   African-American professional baseball player Jackie Robinson is credited with ending decades of segregation in the game when he played first base for the Brooklyn Dodgers in April 1947.

VOGUE

AUG.
$1

02031

our American-look issue

what you wear with what

how to put the great
new separates together

the super new accessories
that make everything work—
head to toe

at last!
wonderful skirts are back

your makeup your hair

ways you'll want to look this fall

good health, good skin,
relaxation, vigor— all in the bath

find your own best looks

play our surprise
clip-and-flip-the-pages game

get the most out of your summer:
tips from famous trend-setters

urgent advice on lifetime health care

PUNK

JANUARY 1976

Publisher: G E Dunn, Jr
Editor: John Holmstrom
Cover illustration and design:
  John Holmstrom
Resident punk: Eddy "Legs" McNeil
English correspondent: Mary Harron

Developed by G E Dunn, Jr, Eddy McNeil and John Holmstrom in autumn 1975, *Punk* – "a combination between Andy Warhol's *Interview* and *Mad* magazine"[1] – quickly came to embody the underground music scene coming out of New York's CBGB club. The catalyst was a Ramones gig there on 23 November. Lou Reed was in the audience.

JOHN HOLMSTROM:

I had seen the Ramones in the summer and loved them immediately. I felt like I had seen the Beatles at the Cavern Club. I thought they could be the first cover. Legs, Mary and I went to their CBGB gig.

MARY HARRON:

I always felt this excitement when I got near CBGB. You'd walk past boarded-up buildings, the Bowery bums, the welfare hotel that was next door. It was like our clubhouse. That was the funny thing: it was threatening yet friendly. It did provide this shelter from the storm. We always used to say everyone there was unpopular at high school. They had been the weirdos and outsiders.

JOHN HOLMSTROM:

There was no one there so we got the front-row table all to ourselves. After the show, we talked to the Ramones but they were horrible. Tommy and Johnny treated us like the enemy. That's why they didn't get the cover.

    Legs was schmoozing their manager, Danny Fields, who said Lou Reed was in the audience. Would we like to interview him? Oh my God, yes! I was a big fan of Velvet Underground and Lou's *Metal Machine Music*, the ultimate punk rock statement, had just come out. I actually had it in quadraphonic, which impressed Lou. He didn't even have it himself. I asked him right off the bat about comic books. I think it disarmed him but it turned out he read EC Comics and knew the names of the artists like, Wally Wood and Will Elder.[2]

I had a lot of difficulty with the cover. I wanted to make Lou look like an insect. That's where the bug eyes came from. I tried antennae and butterfly wings but they didn't work, so I decided to make it look like an EC comic book as much as possible: to suggest horror, but not overstate it. The cult magazine *Famous Monsters of Filmland* was another big influence: all that cheesy Grade B stuff was grist for the mill. My inspiration for the logo and the lettering was the underground cartoonist Vaughn Bodē, who died right when *Punk* was starting. And a lot of fanzines then used a golf-ball typewriter but I hated that look. I was a cartoonist, so I figured I could hand-letter everything, and that became our style.

We brought out the perfect first issue and then it was a long slow slide downhill into oblivion. The punk movement only lasted a few years, but I guess it was only meant to.

1 Mary Harron to Ian Birch, 19 March 2017.
2 Both Wood and Elder had been founding cartoonists on *Mad* magazine when it launched in 1952.

NEW YORK

7 JUNE 1976

Editor: Clay Felker

Design director: Milton Glaser

Art director: Walter Bernard

Cover painting: "Ritual dances of the New
   Saturday Night", detail from a painting by
   James McMullan

In 1976, when entertainment mogul Robert Stigwood saw Nik Cohn's story about an emerging disco culture in working-class Bay Ridge, Brooklyn, he bought the film rights, thinking it would be an ideal project for John Travolta and the then-ailing Bee Gees, both of whom he had under contract. Vincent, the Italian-American teenager in Cohn's story, became Tony Manero (Travolta) in *Saturday Night Fever*, released the following year.

In December 1997 Cohn admitted in *New York* that Vincent had not existed; he was a composite of a gang member from Cohn's youth in Derry/Londonderry and a mod called Chris he had met in London's Shepherd's Bush in 1965. The club, 2001 Odyssey, was real but very different from Cohn's depiction. He confessed, "I knew nothing about this world. Quite literally, I didn't speak the language. So I faked it. There was no excuse for it ... I knew the rules of magazine reporting, and I knew that I was breaking them."

JAMES MCMULLAN:

Nik and I were accompanied to Brooklyn by an African-American guy called "Toute Suite"[1] who had just won a big dance competition. At the time, I thought, "Nik has a thesis about these clubs, this music and he's got this black dancer who sees it from the inside," but as I spent time with them, they were not much more expert on what was happening than I was.

It was basically an Italian supper club and the owners had tried to turn it into this futuristic club on a very limited budget, so it was all about Christmas lights and pieces of Mylar on the walls. I had to use flash, so stuff that was hidden in the darkness got revealed in the photography. I did a painting of a young girl sitting alone in a booth and she was so obviously abandoned and feeling like that sort of social outcast we've all felt at some point. I decided to use the flatness that occurs with flash photography so it became the aesthetic of the paintings. I worked on them a long time. I felt I was doing something high level.

Clay said, "There's no drama here, no knife fights." I began to explain that I felt they were very emotional, and a real human record. Milton said, "Jim, just go outside for a minute and let me talk to Clay." Milton told him that they were not only great illustrations, but ground-breaking.

I finished the paintings but Nik was going through a writer's block about the story and still hadn't written it. I got so worried that the thing would never run that I wrote a story myself and showed it to Milton and Clay. I guess Clay then put a little more pressure on Nik and he finished it.

These were not illustrations in the usual sense because they did not illustrate Nik's story, which was quite different. *New York* ran a disclaimer, saying that my paintings were made up but that Nik's story was true.

It was Nik's story rather than a story of that disco. And it was a good story. He got a big payday: $500,000 which in those years was huge. I think he wrote a treatment for the movie, which they didn't use. I got nothing. I didn't press the issue, even though Nik told me that Stigwood was really impressed with the paintings and that he might not have read the article had it not been for them.

1 Sometimes written as "Tu Sweet".

Nigel Dempster, the World's Boldest Gossip
Governor Carey Hits Rock Bottom, by Ken Auletta
The Mid-Life Crises of 'Time' and 'Newsweek'

75 CENTS   JUNE 7, 1976

New York

Tribal Rites of the New Saturday Night
By Nik Cohn

VOGUE

FEB
60p

the fresh taste of spring

racing green
how to wear it
and **what to wear** with what

prettiest new
make-up
colours

tops and tunics
with more dash than cash

springboard to
health
new diets, new exercises,
new you

who's reading what?
the bedside reading guide

VOGUE

FEBRUARY 1977

Editor: Beatrix Miller

Art director: Terry Jones

Cover photography: Willie Christie

Fashion editor: Grace Coddington

Make-up: Barbara Daly

Cover credit: "Rowntree's jelly ... full of gelatine, a valuable source of protein and good for strengthening nails."

British *Vogue*'s art director Terry Jones loved to subvert. Here he breaks every rule for a fashion glossy: don't show food (and certainly never show someone eating it); don't use green (because it doesn't sell); and always have eye contact.

TERRY JONES:

I hated covers that were shot as covers. This was a beauty shot done for a colour promotion. Twice a year *Vogue* had colour promotions, and green was the colour this time. Grace had done the shot with Willie Christie, who she was married to at the time, and had put this as an inside shot. I thought, I'm going to push this and somehow Bea and the distributor agreed. We didn't run it past Liberman[1] but we did ask Bernie Leser, the UK managing director, who had only been in the job for six months. He said, "Go for it." But when it was on press Daniel Salem, the European president, saw it and screamed, "Get it off the press. It's not a *Vogue* cover." It was so far removed from anything that had been done before but it was too late. It went on sale and was the fastest-selling issue that year.

Bea gave me the support to do something different. To everyone else, she appeared fearsome but I never found her fearsome. I found her really good to work with. As creative director, you have to feed an editor ideas so the idea becomes theirs. The battle was always with the production department. They are the blockage between the creative and the printer. The printer will accept the challenge.

WILLIE CHRISTIE:

All the props were green – a little green acrobatic airplane, a green table tennis bat, a green surfboard and the jelly. Marcie Hunt was the model and I shot a Polaroid of her in a green shirt and green baseball-type hat. Grace then said, "We're going to have her eating green jelly." We put it together but it just didn't work (*see* Figure 9). We didn't shoot any film of this version. I am sure you can see why! Then someone said, "Let's go in for a close-up." I had a 150 Hasselblad and went in tighter, tighter, tighter. We had no idea this would be a cover. When we saw the mock-up, we thought, "Bloody hell, that's amazing." The picture is like an abstract art piece, really.

Figure 9 Christie's original polaroid.

---

1   Alexander Liberman, then editorial director of Condé Nast Publications, United States and Europe, based in New York.

RADIO TIMES

11–17 JUNE 1977

Editor: Geoffrey Cannon

Art director: David Driver

Cover drawing: Dennis Lillee by
Ralph Steadman (16 March 1977)

By 1969 *Radio Times* had "degenerated into a publicity sheet for mass-market entertainment programmes".[1] The owners, BBC Publications, wanted change, and that came in September when Geoffrey Cannon and David Driver staged a virtual coup with their new editorial vision that lasted for over a decade. They created a hugely successful quality and inventively designed general interest magazine built around comprehensive TV and radio listings.

In March 1977 they sent artist Ralph Steadman to Melbourne to cover the Centenary Test between England and Australia. Australia won by 45 runs, the victory secured in large part by the magical relationship between bowler Dennis Lillee and wicket-keeper Rod Marsh. Steadman took a small sketchbook and camera. "I probably used my little Minox." Four years later, he recalled: "As he ran up to bowl, the people in the cheap stand were chanting 'Lillee, Lillee, Lillee': it was a sort of death ritual. There is always a stillness as the ball leaves the bowler's hand, people waiting, and then, if the ball is hit, the seagulls around the pitch take off like the souls of the dead in an Aztec sacrifice. That moment was the one I had to get, that moment of hushed violence. What I was drawing would probably cause me great trouble, because they were not sports drawings in the ordinary sense, they were pretty strong social comments."[2]

The cover brilliantly captured "that moment". It also announced the first Test match in the Ashes series at Lord's but Lillee was no longer in the Australian team.

GEOFFREY CANNON:

This is David's story. Choosing Ralph Steadman to cover cricket was an inspiration. The violence in modern cricket had never been portrayed like this. It was a revolutionary cover, no doubt, which I guess would be in anybody's top-ten *Radio Times* covers.

DAVID DRIVER:

I was told we couldn't afford to send him to Australia, but Ralph said, "I have a student card so I can get a cheap ticket. I really want to do it." Ralph didn't know

LONDON (BBC Radio London: page 54) 11-17 June 1977   Price 12p

RadioTimes

Fast and furious

There's no Lillee this time
— so can England tame the Aussie
demon bowlers in the
Jubilee Test? Full coverage
from Thursday BBCtv
and Radio 3. Back feature:
Radio Times asks is
cricket a game — or war?

much about cricket so I gave him a full briefing. I knew he would just love the tone, the texture, the atmosphere. I knew he'd tear into it, and he did. He came back thrilled with the experience and did these wonderful drawings. Then the Australians came here three months later for the Jubilee Test. This was the Ashes and it was a real personality-packed confrontation between England and Australia. It was very aggressive, very bloody. The Australians loved Ralph's drawings and wanted to buy them, and I think many of them did.

RALPH STEADMAN:

Learning about cricket was the attraction. I first looked at WD Grace and the history of the game. I even went to the Oval to soak up the atmosphere. I got interested in the spectators, as I had at the Kentucky Derby.[3] The crowd is fascinating – the interaction between spectators and players.

[The English and Australians] were all intent on winning and therefore they expressed their inner determination, not in anger, but with more exertion than normal people. You are hurling a ball down at someone with a wooden bat; it's like a bullet. It's a bit alarming. I always hope someone catches it instead of being hit in the face. I played school cricket and you could be a slow-spin ball bowler so it would drop and bounce one way, and not the other, and confuse the batsman. It's an unknown quantity. The ball can do something surprising.

I was intrigued by the fact that people actually got so fascinated by it. I wanted to understand that obsession. I don't know how the readership reacted. No one told me that. They were far too frightened.

1 Geoffrey Cannon email interview with Ian Birch, August 2016.
2 Quoted from David Driver (ed.), *The Art of Radio Times: First Sixty Years*, BBC Publications, 1981, p.225. Interview by Peter Harle. Reproduced with kind permission from David Driver.
3 The legendary essay, "The Kentucky Derby is Decadent and Depraved, written under duress by Hunter S. Thompson, sketched with eyebrow pencil and lipstick by Ralph Steadman", *Scanlan's Monthly*, vol. 1, no. 4, June 1970.

SOUNDS

25 MARCH 1978

Editor: Alan Lewis

Features editor: Vivien Goldman

Cover feature: "It Can't Happen Here
Or Can It?" was the result of work by
Phil Sutcliffe, Caroline Coon,
Vivien Goldman, Jon Savage,
Pete Silverton, SOUNDS editorial
staff and Rock Against Racism.

By 1978 the grassroots movement Rock Against Racism (RAR) had become an important rallying point for countering the growing racial tension in Britain, and the neo-fascist National Front (NF), in particular. Vivien Goldman, a tireless champion of black music, decided *Sounds* had to take a stand. The cover and report inside were timely: RAR and the Anti-Nazi League were planning a London march culminating in an open-air music festival in Victoria Park on 30 April. Around 100,000 people would turn up.

CAROLINE COON:

"It Can't Happen Here" was a spontaneous demonstration: we felt a real sense of responsibility that we could make a difference. You can't be a rock and roll magazine and allow racism.

I said, "I'm going to interview Martin Webster." He was the National Activities Organizer for the National Front. I just rang him up. He'd heard of me and said, "Yes, come along". I did a lot of research and went with a stack of hard questions. Interviewing this racist was almost like a Monty Python sketch: it is so out of rational bounds that it becomes comedy.

I thought, I'm going to expose this bastard and deliver the best copy I can to Vivien. At one point I asked him, "If your policies are taken to their logical conclusion, 90 per cent of rock bands in this country will have to be repatriated to various parts of the world." "Yes, that's right," he replied, "And there they can amuse their own people." That drove the idea for the "Deported!" cover treatment. At the end of the interview, I could hardly bear what I'd heard.

I then had to take pictures of him. We were in the front room of his Victorian terrace in Connaught Road, Teddington, which was also the National Front office. I'd taken one picture but the light wasn't quite right. I stood him in another space, closed the door and saw this image of a very beautiful black youth on the back of the door, staring at me. Beside it was a picture of an older black musician who might have been Tapper Zukie – I can't remember. I knew I couldn't point that out to Webster so I quietly took the photograph. He had not wanted me to see it. The other side of the door had a Union Jack on it.

VIVIEN GOLDMAN:
I had the idea and masterminded it, but we wrote it like a commune. Caroline had a very pronounced sense of justice. Afterwards, the feeling was the paper had gone too far in that activist direction and they started to give space to Gary Bushell's Oi! bands that teetered on the edge of NF support. That's when I left *Sounds*. The struggle there was completely debilitating for me. But for a while we had a good run of being the activist face of punk in a much more unmediated way than *Melody Maker* or the *NME*, which were much bigger. We were the feisty, scrappy outsiders.

MARCH 25 1978 18p

TUBES, TELEVISION dates

sounds

**PAUL SIMONON
(CLASH)**

**PHIL LYNOTT
(THIN LIZZY)**

**POLY STYRENE
(X-RAY SPEX)**

**CHARLIE TUMAHAI
(BEBOP DELUXE)**

**GEORGE CSAPO
(BETHNAL)**

**CARL LEVY
(CIMARONS)**

**ERROLL BROWN
(HOT CHOCOLATE)**

**ARRI UP
(SLITS)**

**FREDDY MERCURY
(QUEEN)**

**RAY LAKE
(REAL THING)**

**JEAN BURNEL
(STRANGLERS)**

**RITA RAY
(DARTS)**

IS THIS THE FUTURE
OF ROCK 'N' ROLL ?

RACISM AND YOUR MUSIC — FACE TO FACE WITH THE FRONT

SPECIAL REPORT Pages 25-33

1980s

RAW

LAUNCH ISSUE, JULY 1980

Editors/publishers: Françoise Mouly
    & Art Spiegelman
Cover drawing: Art Spiegelman

By the late 1970s the underground comics scene was languishing: it was about to be re-energized by a new personal and professional partnership. Paris-born ex-architecture student and comics enthusiast Françoise Mouly had come to New York and met then unknown American cartoonist Art Spiegelman. Together they created *Raw*, a new "graphix magazine". *Raw* would champion visionary artists, showcase European comics and revolutionize the graphic novel when it introduced *Maus*, Spiegelman's Pulitzer Prize-winning work about surviving the Holocaust.

FRANÇOISE MOULY:

I wanted to bring together all that I discovered when I met Art. With me discovering American comics and Art discovering European comics, we wanted to put the two together. Furthermore, I had been shocked by the prejudices against comics in America: comics, it seemed, were for idiots. I didn't think that.

I had conversations with friends of Art's, such as Robert Crumb, who were adamant that the medium should remain the domain of throwaway and disposable publications on newsprint. I didn't want *Raw* to be thrown away. I wanted to find a middle ground between the expensive limited-edition art object and the throwaway underground comic. The first issue was intended to be a departure from everything else that was around at the time.

Art's inspiration in wanting to be a cartoonist was discovering the early *Mad* magazine – and that was true for many underground cartoonists – so a short, one-word name was important. *Raw* was meant in the sense of "uncooked", the

VOLUME 1 NUMBER 1 $3.50

IN THIS ISSUE:

ALFRED JARRY : HOMMAGES POSTHUMES

ART SPIEGELMAN : TWO-FISTED PAINTERS

JACQUES TARDI : MANHATTAN

THE GRAPHIX MAGAZINE OF POSTPONED SUICIDES

opposite of slick. I think Art chose the name because I couldn't pronounce it. It made him laugh to hear me say *Raw*.

I was pretty much able to do everything myself, so I didn't have to pay a staff. I was publisher. I put up the money. I got it printed. I did the distribution. I wanted a large-size format,[1] in part because in the independent bookstores at the time there were large-size magazines like *WET*, *Metropolis* and, later, *Émigré*. A lot of them were on newsprint, but I wanted good paper. So *Raw* was expensive compared to other comics: the first issue was $3.50 when other comics were a dollar.

When you launch a magazine, the one constant is the logo. We did the opposite. We changed the logo with every issue. It was designed by whoever did the cover. And we changed the subtitle every issue. The first issue is called *The Graphix Magazine of Postponed Suicides* with Art's drawing of someone jumping out of a window. It's from a quote by the philosopher E M Cioran[2] that Art and I liked very much: "A book is a postponed suicide."[3] It also functioned as our answer to many people who thought, "Oh, *Raw* is so depressing and dark."

I couldn't afford colour printing so I ran off a signature of colour panels of Art's drawing and we glued one to each cover, with Elmer's Glue. The quantities were manageable: the print run was 3,500 copies. It was very important to me that each issue remain a handmade product even though it was printed.

1 The first issue of *Raw* was 10½ inches × 14⅛ inches (27cm × 36cm).
2 Romanian philosopher who lived much of his life in Paris.
3 Quoted from "The Trouble with Being Born", *Raw*, vol. 1, issue 1 (July 1980), contents page.

i-D

LAUNCH ISSUE, AUGUST/SEPTEMBER 1980

Editors: Perry Haines, Terry Jones,
   Al McDowell
Special thanks to i-D photographer
   Steve Johnson, Ed Gillan, i-D stylist
   Caroline Baker, Anne Witchard and Trish.

Terry Jones launched *i-D* as a quarterly out of his house in north-west London a few months after the first issue of *The Face*. With a battle cry of "Fans, not critics", it championed street style both in its content (pared-down, head-to-toe portraits of "fans" with micro interviews that Jones called "Straight Up") and in its design (the landscape-shaped, handmade fanzine format). The logo was inspired, suggesting a winking eye and smiling face, and presaging the world of emoticons.

TERRY JONES:

Back in 1976 I had been discussing with Toscani[1] and Caroline Baker how the fashion world needed a new type of magazine. We were going to do something called *The Whole World Clothes Catalogue* but it never happened. The idea was that it would an international base for exchanging information – even as far as if you're going on holiday, you don't need a suitcase because you have found someone who is your size, and thinks like you, and you can use their wardrobe.

CAROLINE BAKER:

It was a bit of a clothes Airbnb but with no money involved. Toscani was very politically driven. So was Terry in a more subtle, visual way. Anti-bourgeoisie, into street style and the people.

TERRY JONES:

Right from the start, I wanted to create something that would become a collectable and not landfill. I wanted *i-D* to feel like a social document, so the

FASHION MAGAZINE Nº1 50p

i-D

street photography inside was about documenting that moment. "Straight up" is a Bristolian phrase. It's about asking a question and getting a straight answer, no messing.

The photographer was the journalist. Steve Johnson, who did the punk book[2] with me, was one of the key people to do the photos. He hated getting words from people, so invariably someone had to be there to take down the words. That was how Dylan Jones, Alex Sharkey and Caryn Franklin would start their careers.

There was also the idea that everyone's a star: the Warhol "15 minutes of fame" concept. It was democratizing and it was about style as opposed to fashion. Calling ourselves a "fashion magazine" was tongue-in-cheek: we had nothing to do with the business of fashion. It was about infiltrating the mainstream.

Every cover of *i-D* 1 and 2 was a unique piece because the fanzine printer, Better Badges, had never done a two-colour job like that before. So the chances of getting it in register were virtually zero. It went from fire engine red to rouge pink. It was meant to be fluoro pink but they would just tip the ink in. Knowing that you're not going to get a perfect result is what interests me.

I wanted to have it so there was no photographic image. It was about the concept of identity, your ID. And iD were the initials of my studio then, "informat Designer", always with a lowercase "i" because I was a fan of e e cummings.

The lowercase "i" for *i-D* created a face so, when you turned it around, it was a graphic of a winking eye and a smiling face. I could appropriate all the other things that the wink implies: seductive, in the know. There was also a hidden side: the closed eye. I wanted something as strong as the Playboy bunny.

1 The photographer Oliviero Toscani, *see Colors* (page 148)
2 Terry Jones and Isabelle Anscombe, *Not Another Punk Book*, Aurum Press, 1978.

ROLLING STONE

22 JANUARY 1981

Editor and publisher: Jann S Wenner

Chief photographer: Annie Leibovitz

Cover photograph: Annie Leibovitz, John Lennon and Yoko Ono in the "Morning Room" of their New York City apartment, early afternoon, 8 December 1980

Annie Leibovitz had memorably photographed John Lennon at the start of her career for a haunting cover in 1971.[1] Almost ten years later to the day, she walked into Lennon and Yoko Ono's seventh-floor apartment in the Dakota to do two sessions with them – on Wednesday 3 December, and Monday 8 December.

Leibovitz wanted to capture them in an embrace. Lennon was keen, Ono was not happy to lose her clothes, so Leibovitz suggested that she leave everything on, as a contrast. She took a Polaroid. When Lennon saw it, he said, "You've captured our relationship exactly."

He told Leibovitz how important it was for Yoko to be on the cover as well. "I promised John that this would be the cover. I looked him in the eye and we shook on it."[2] They planned to meet up later to review the transparencies. It didn't happen.

That Monday evening Lennon was shot by Mark Chapman outside The Dakota and pronounced dead at 11.07pm. Wenner was devastated. When he saw the pictures the next day, "My eye went right to it and John had said that's the one they wanted, too." Cover lines weren't necessary.

The issue was a remarkable memorial, sold a massive 1.45 million copies and helped shape Lennon's legacy. In 2005 the American Society of Magazine Editors voted it the number one magazine cover to appear since 1965.

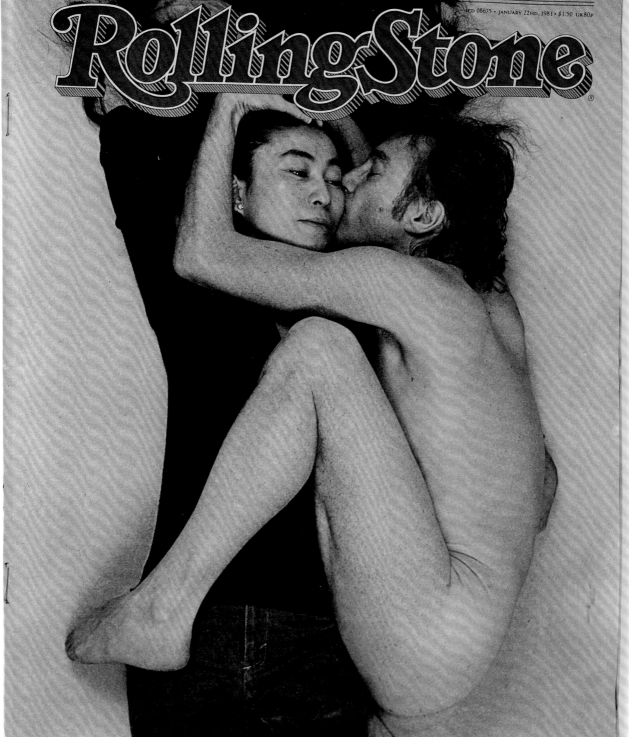

ICD 08675 • JANUARY 22ND, 1981 • $1.50 UK80P

RollingStone

JANN WENNER:

That image is just so resonant and rich with their own relationship and ideas and philosophy about life. Then the events of the day made it so incredibly powerful; it took on this other life on top of that. You see all the overtones of death and rebirth. It inadvertently portrayed the forthcoming moment. There's the art of it, and then there's the message of it, which is extraordinarily powerful, and then there is the prophetic nature of it.

I don't know where you find that combination of events: a great photographer, the moment, and all that stuff. I've never seen another cover of a magazine, ours or any other, quite as strong as that. The issue itself was done at the moment. It's right from the moment and, given who he was and who he was to us, it was one from the heart and I think that that heart is all over that issue. It's wounded, and it's bleeding, and it's in agony and it's full of love. You have the last official image of the two of them ever. It was both personal as well as professional. We had our job to do but we had our love to express.

John Lennon really helped get *Rolling Stone* off the ground in various ways. He was on the first cover, but more than that he gave us that kind of interview and that kind of access and that kind of news that built the magazine's reputation and name recognition again and again and again, whether it was the "Two Virgins" cover or the famous "Lennon Remembers" interview. He just opened up, whereas the Beatles had been so hermetically sealed off. We kind of became his official media spokesman for as long as he was alive.

1   *Rolling Stone*, 21 January 1971.
2   *Rolling Stone*, 22 January 1981, contents page.

THE FACE

MARCH 1985

Publisher/editor: Nick Logan
Art director: Neville Brody
Design: Neville Brody & Robin Derrick
Cover photography: Jamie Morgan
Styling: Ray Petri
Cover model: Felix Howard[1]

Eighties fashion saw the rise of the stylist, and Ray Petri led the charge. He invented the decade's young urban male uniform – MA1 jacket with orange lining, Levi's 501 jeans, white socks and Dr. Martens loafers. Petri's trademark "Buffalo" look was showcased in six influential shoots he did for *The Face* with photographer Jamie Morgan. This was one of them: Petri and Morgan lashed together classic tailoring with post-punk street style.

JAMIE MORGAN:

The word "Buffalo" was just right for us for many reasons. The rude-boy attitude was a big part of it, as was Bob Marley's song "Buffalo Soldier", talking about the black slaves taken to America. Also, the buffalo in Native American culture was honoured: it was used to clothe and feed a community. Then the white man destroys the culture and kills all the buffalo. To us, the American Indians and the buffalo represent the underdog, the cultural outsider. This was us. We all came from immigrant or mixed-race families. We kicked against the white establishment and the fashion industry – not in any heavy way – because we were not represented in establishment fashion magazines.

NICK LOGAN:

It was a golden day when Ray came through the door with Jamie. They had a couple of shots of Nick and Barry Kamen and it grew from that. We had a kind of ad hoc arrangement. As footballers will say, it's one game at a time. We'd just say yes to their next thing; we didn't need to talk about it.

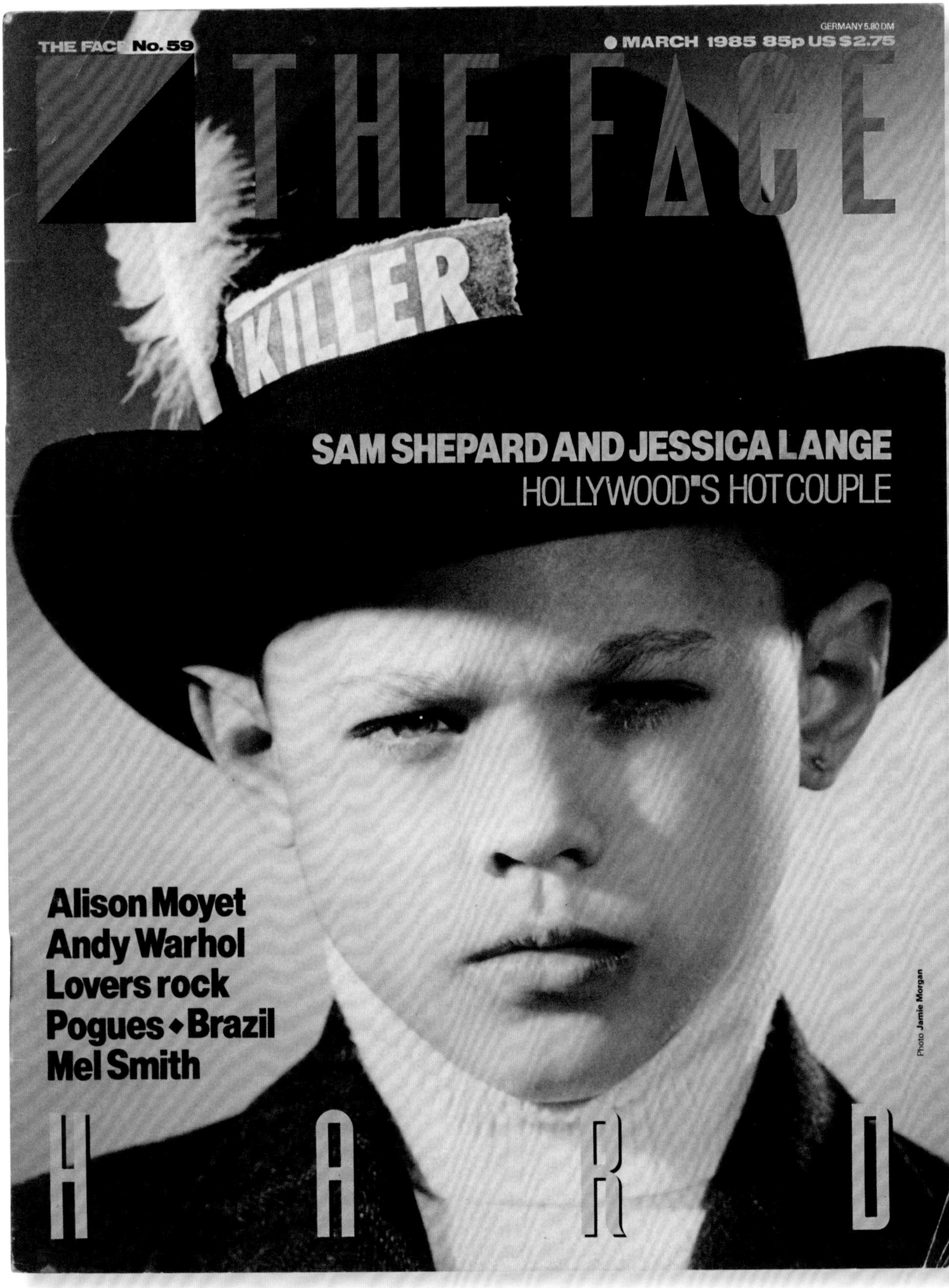

GERMANY 5.80 DM

THE FACE No. 59

● MARCH 1985 85p US $2.75

THE FACE

KILLER

SAM SHEPARD AND JESSICA LANGE
HOLLYWOOD'S HOT COUPLE

**Alison Moyet
Andy Warhol
Lovers rock
Pogues ◆ Brazil
Mel Smith**

HARD

Photo Jamie Morgan

JAMIE MORGAN:

The clothes were never our main concern. We always started with casting and a cultural or artistic point of view. We wanted to reclaim the idea that men are often far more flamboyant than women.

NICK LOGAN:

I needed persuading to run the "Killer" cover. I was a bit apprehensive about how it would be received, what it said about us, because Felix was only 12. And the word "killer", which was just torn out of a newspaper. But it looked fantastic and everybody in the office loved it. It's probably my favourite cover of *The Face*.

JAMIE MORGAN:

Felix was the son of a friend of Ray's. I just loved his face – that it was old and young, powerful and vulnerable, at the same time. This type of casting had no precedent and I wasn't sure people would get it.

We spent time in Jamaica partly because of the West London Jamaican community that we enjoyed so much and because we were working with reggae artists like Gregory Isaacs and Freddie McGregor. The words "killer", "hard" and "wicked" were all used in Jamaica and soon became part of London slang. I like to think we were part of the London cultural melting pot.

ROBIN DERRICK:

The magazine came out on Tuesday, and on Thursday I was in some nightclub, Do-Do's or The Wag, and people had newspaper headlines pinned to their clothes. It was extraordinary: it was that literal and that direct. Everyone knew where the idea came from. It was cool to copy *The Face*.

---

1 The following year Felix Howard appeared in Madonna's video for "Open Your Heart" and later he became a successful songwriter and music business executive.

NATIONAL GEOGRAPHIC

JUNE 1985

Editor: Bill Garrett

Cover subject: Sharbat Gula

Cover photography: Steve McCurry

In 1984 American photographer Steve McCurry was at the Afghanistan–Pakistan border, researching a story for *National Geographic* about the flood of refugees from Afghanistan, triggered by the Soviet invasion, when he spotted this 12-year-old orphan. She was deeply traumatized. Her village had been bombed and her parents killed; with her grandmother, brother and three sisters, she had walked for weeks in the middle of winter across the mountains to reach the camp. The photograph came to represent the complex emotions of the refugee – suffering, determination, defiance and dignity.

STEVE McCURRY:

I was in the Nasir Bagh refugee camp outside of Peshawar and came across a tent that was being used as an elementary school for girls. I noticed this little girl with beautiful eyes in the corner of the tent, looking haunted. There was something unique and disturbing about her. This was a girl of simple means but she was holding her head high. I literally had a couple of minutes with her before she walked away, but everything worked – the light, her expression, the background, the shawl.

There's an authenticity to this picture. She's giving you exactly what is inside of her. I didn't speak Pashtun, her language; she didn't speak English and this was the first time she had been photographed. She wasn't sure what a portrait was. Who knows what was going through her mind and how much of that look was curiosity at me and the camera? She has an expression which is sort of neutral but with a hint of something positive.

There were two possible versions for the cover: one of her looking at the camera and one with her hand on her face. The picture editor at the time thought the one looking at the camera was too disturbing. He didn't want to show it to the editor, Bill Garrett. So we compromised: we'd show him both. Bill literally leapt to his feet when he saw the direct gaze and said, "There's our cover."

After 9/11, when the world's attention once again turned to Afghanistan, I wanted to go back again to find her. I never knew her name or any details about her. So in January 2002, I went with a team from *National Geographic* and we found her, living in the Tora Bora region. Her name was Sharbat Gula.

When I first saw her again, it was a bit of a shock. My reference was her at 12, not a woman around 30, married and a mother of three children.

We didn't embrace: it's just out of the question. But we did a second cover.[1] I photographed her in her burka holding the original picture.

That original picture has been reproduced millions of times as advertising for *National Geographic*. The ethics are clear: you don't want to be accused of exploiting an orphan who happens to be a refugee. Initially, compensation came from *National Geographic*,[2] but then I bought her a house. My sister Bonnie and I also started a non-profit called ImagineAsia.[3] We wanted to take some dramatic steps to make her life better.

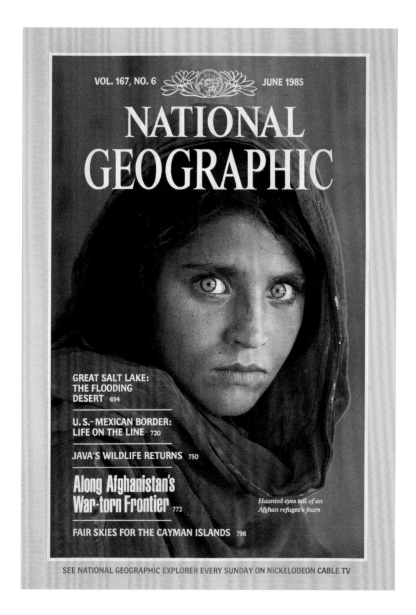

VOL. 167, NO. 6   JUNE 1985

NATIONAL GEOGRAPHIC

GREAT SALT LAKE: THE FLOODING DESERT 694

U.S.–MEXICAN BORDER: LIFE ON THE LINE 720

JAVA'S WILDLIFE RETURNS 750

Along Afghanistan's War-torn Frontier 772

Haunted eyes tell of an Afghan refugee's fears

FAIR SKIES FOR THE CAYMAN ISLANDS 798

SEE NATIONAL GEOGRAPHIC EXPLORER EVERY SUNDAY ON NICKELODEON CABLE TV

1 April 2002.
2 It established the Afghan Girls Fund in 2002 when the expulsion of the Taliban made it possible for girls to seek education, a right they had long been denied under Taliban rule. In 2008 it was extended to boys and given a new name, the Afghan Children's Fund.
3 ImagineAsia works in partnership with local community leaders and regional NGOs to help provide educational resources and opportunities to children in Afghanistan.

ELLE

OTTOBRE 1987

NUMERO
UNO
SPECIALE
L. 2000

SCOPRI
IL TUO
MODO DI
AMARE

VIAGGIO
A SUD
DI CAPO
NORD

IL RACCONTO
DI **ELLE**,
UN INEDITO
DI McINERNEY

QUALI SONO
LE NUOVE
VIRTÙ

IL PUNTO SULLO
STILE
90 PAGINE DI MODA

ITALIA L. 4000 FRANCIA F. 30 GERMANIA DM. 11 GRAN BRETAGNA LGS 2.80 SPAGNA PTAS 550 SVIZZERA FRS 7.80 SVIZZERA CANTON TICINO FRS 7.50 USA $ 4.50

ITALIAN ELLE

LAUNCH ISSUE, OCTOBER 1987
NOVEMBER 1987
DECEMBER 1987
JANUARY 1988 (PROPOSED COVER IMAGE, NEVER PUBLISHED)
Editor-in-chief: Carla Sozzani
Managing editor: Eugenio Gallavotti
Art director: Robin Derrick

Italian *Elle*, published in a joint venture between Hachette and Rizzoli, was a departure from the brand's template. Carla Sozzani brought a level of experimentation that Hachette did not usually allow. But the big five Italian fashion houses grew seriously rattled when Sozzani didn't feature their product on the covers. Sozzani and art director Robin Derrick were fired after three issues.

ROBIN DERRICK:
Carla called me and said, "Will you do Italian *Elle*?" I was the art director of *The Face* and had just taken over from Neville [Brody] who was doing *Arena*.

I brought my kind of "cool" *Face* and *i-D* photographers who had yet to make their name like Nick Knight and Juergen Teller. Carla brought photographers from her *Vogue* background like Steven Meisel, Bruce Weber, Paolo Roversi. It was an amazing combination. Carla and I were really aligned. We laughed so much. Carla had this line, "*Ogni giorno una festa*" – every day's a party.

CARLA SOZZANI:
Nick Knight photographed the first cover. I wanted something that was purer in shape and look. The red turtleneck is Benetton and coat Montana. This collection was very clean and simple, almost severe – a little bit like my vision, super-minimal. We chose red, green and white because they were the colours of the Italian flag.

ROBIN DERRICK:
I loved the first cover but the difference between it and the weekly French *Elle* was too big. You could start to see the mismatch.

EUGENIO GALLAVOTTI:
The first issue sold out. We had more difficulties with the next issues.

CARLA SOZZANI:
Nick did the November cover as well and we had the Japanese model Maki Shibuya. For December, I asked Christian Lacroix if I could have a pattern for an evening dress from his last couture collection and put it in *Elle* so everyone

ELLE

NOVEMBRE

L. 4000

ESCLUSIVO
ELLE IN
RUSSIA
COSA STA
CAMBIANDO

**NUCLEARE
SÌ O NO**
DUE
SCIENZIATE A
CONFRONTO

LA MODA
DEGLI OPPOSTI
**MASCHILE
O FEMMINILE**

IL CORPO SOTTILE E

SENSUALE

ANNO 1 - N. 2 -

CANADA $ 5.95 FRANCIA F. 30 GERMANIA DM. 11 GRAN BRETAGNA LGS ... 650 SPAGNA PTAS 550 SVIZZERA FRS 7.80 SVIZZERA CANTON TICINO FRS 7.50 US

ELLE

DICEMBRE

L. 4000

GUIDA A UN GRANDE NATALE
LA MODA, I REGALI, LE RICETTE

IN **ESCLUSIVA**
PER LE LETTRICI
DI **ELLE** UNO
SPLENDIDO ABITO
DA SERA DI
ALTA MODA

CURARSI
CON IL
SONNO

SPECIALE
DENARO
COME E
QUANTO
INVESTIRE

INCHIESTA: CHE COS'È OGGI
L'AMORE

ANNO I - N. 3 - SPEDIZ. ABB. POST. GR. III/70
CANADA $ 5.95 FRANCIA F. 30 GERMANIA DM. 11 GRAN BRETAGNA LGS 2.80 GRECIA DRS 650 SPAGNA PTAS 550 SVIZZERA FRS 7.80 SVIZZERA CANTON TICINO FRS 7.50 USA N.Y.C $ 4.50 OTHER $ 4.95

could make the dress. The model, Meg Grosswendt, is wearing the dress on the cover. Paolo Roversi took the photograph. I wanted to do another cover with him with a dress by Alaïa but they fired me before it came out.

They offered me an interesting amount of money to say I was leaving but I said, "Why? You are firing me. I am not ashamed, and anyway Diana Vreeland[1] had been fired from *Vogue*." They said, "Who is Diana Vreeland?" and I said, "There is one more reason for you to fire me. If you don't know who she is, we have no point of communication."

ROBIN DERRICK:

I knew I was being fired when the *fattorino* [office boy], who would come around with the post on a trolley, came into my office and started taking the magazine layouts down from the wall. The guy was deaf and dumb, so I couldn't talk to him.

My understanding is that they had received a telegram from the trading group for brands like Armani and Valentino. They said, unless the editorial direction of the magazine changed and featured more Italian clothes, they were going to withdraw their advertising – not just from *Elle* but from all the magazines in the Rizzoli Group. I was told at the time that that was $32 million worth of advertising. They fired Carla and me that day.

Our *Elle* was really up there, and beyond. We did three iconic issues: they were art pieces.

---

1 Fashion legend who was fashion editor at American *Harper's Bazaar* before becoming editor-in-chief of American *Vogue* in 1963. She was fired in 1971.

ELLE

THE NICE NEW YORK MONTHLY ‣ APRIL $2.50

SPY

Our NICE ISSUE

▲▲▲▲▲▲▲▲▲

DONALD TRUMP
A Heck of a Guy

GLAMOROUS GALS
Who Never Ever Age

IT'S *FUN*
to Live in Queens

PAUL SIMON
Music's Mr. Generosity

0 74470 74128 2

04

SPY

**APRIL 1988
(COVER AND P.1)**

Editors: Graydon Carter & Kurt Anderson
Publisher: Thomas L Phillips Jr.
Executive editor: Susan Morrison
Art director: Alexander Isley
Photographs: Deborah Feingold (body) &
    Joe McNally/Wheeler Pictures (head)

Kurt Andersen and Graydon Carter hatched the idea for *Spy*[1] when they were working at *Time* in the mid-1980s. They wanted an exhaustively researched satirical monthly about "the great commercial machines"[2] that fuelled New York. Launched in October 1986, it was whip-smart, mischievous and sometimes merciless, but always happy to burn bridges as it skewered its privileged subjects. As Tina Brown noted, "It flatters media people by bothering to take them down."[3] *Spy* ridiculed Donald Trump from the first issue and coined the "short-fingered vulgarian" epithet that re-emerged in the rhetoric of the 2017 American presidential campaign. Trump has never forgiven them.

ALEXANDER ISLEY:

We wanted to do an April Fool's issue. *Spy* was getting the reputation of being the snarky bad boy, so, we thought, wouldn't it be fun to make it "Our Nice Issue" and, since Donald Trump had been the bête noire of *Spy* for a long time, do something *good* about him?

I had this idea of doing him with his signature thumbs-up, being "a heck of a guy". Then, when you opened it up, he'd have a red tail like the devil which went across the first spread. It was to telegraph to the world that it was "Our Nice Issue" – but not *really*. But the sales staff went and sold an ad on the spread, so the tail idea didn't work.

We thought, "Why not make it a magazine publishing joke and have the cover lines and barcode collapse instead?" It was Kurt's body, though he didn't want that to come out at the time. Throughout the shoot, Kurt was wise-cracking, saying Trump things like, "This is the best cover there's ever going to be." We had photos of Trump's head blown up and held them in front of Kurt, trying to match the angle and the pose and the light. The colour backgrounds are different on the two pages. It would have been an extra $400 to colour-correct the second image, but the publisher, Tom, said we couldn't do that.

SUSAN MORRISON:

I love that one. The colour palette is very playtime-y.

We didn't think too much then about Trump as a force of evil as much as a giant asshole. That does remind me of a cover we did later about the concept of people who had made Faustian bargains. I got Elvis Costello to be on the cover,[4] posing as the devil. We didn't want it to be someone in a sequined red outfit, so we dressed him in a very tailored suit like a Wall Street Master of the Universe with very subtle horns on his hairline. Costello was leaning forward like a businessman, handing out his card. In very tiny type on the bottom of the card is the phone number of Trump Tower. So, if you called that number, you got the reception of the Trump organization. I don't know if anyone called.

KURT ANDERSEN:

In an issue in 1988[5] we actually conducted a national poll of candidates including Donald Trump. He was at the time, ridiculously it seemed, flirting with the idea of running for president and we found that 4 per cent of Americans wished he were running. I never imagined that 30 years later this magazine, in this accidental, strange way, would have contemporary relevance. He wasn't the only thing we did but he was a major obsession.

1   The magazine's name was inspired by caricaturist Leslie Ward, who worked for Vanity Fair in the early 1900s under the pseudonym "Spy".
2   Graydon Carter, in Kurt Andersen, Graydon Carter and George Kalogerakis, *Spy: The Funny Years*, Miramax Books, 2006, p.5.
3   Tina Brown, *The Vanity Fair Diaries*, 1983–1992, Weidenfeld & Nicolson, 2017, p.346.
4   June 1989.
5   January–February 1988. Headlined "Nation to Trump: We Need You", the issue was part of *Spy*'s "Route 88 Campaign Manual".

1990s

THE FACE

No 22/JULY 1990 £1.50 • US $4.75
ITALY L5500 GERMANY 9.5DM SPAIN 435PTAS BELG. 105 BFR

THE 3RD SUMMER OF LOVE

Stone Roses on Spike Island, an A-Z of the new bands, Daisy Age fashion, Hendrix and psychedelia

'Kiss my butt!' Sandra on Madonna

Prince in Minneapolis: tour preview

Indian summer: photography Corinne Day

JOHN WATERS / MICKEY ROURKE / MARSHALL JEFFERSON / TIM ROTH

0 74470 72689 0   07

THE FACE

JULY 1990

Editor/publisher: Nick Logan

Assistant editor/features editor:
   Sheryl Garratt

Art director: Phil Bicker

Cover photographer: Corinne Day

Stylist: Melanie Ward at Z Agency

Model: Kate Moss at Storm

This was the cover that lit the fuse for Kate Moss.

PHIL BICKER:

I was trying to find a model who was the embodiment of *The Face*. It was the era of supermodels – Linda Evangelista, Cindy Crawford, Tatjana Patitz, Christy Turlington – but they all felt inaccessible and didn't have any real relationship to what *The Face* was doing. Photographer Corinne Day, who had been a model herself, came to see me with a fashion test shoot, half a dozen black-and-white prints and some contact sheets. Among the prints was an image of this young girl walking along the motorway in Ickenham, north-west London. As someone who'd grown up in the same London suburbs as Corinne, I connected with the setting of the photo and particularly to the model, Kate, who looked relatable, natural and authentic.

I think Corinne saw herself in Kate. Kate became her muse. I ran the single image in *The Face* a couple months later as part of a portfolio that featured the first published photos by Corinne, David Sims and Glen Luchford. Then Corinne and I started to work on ideas for a full Kate story.

Corinne went to Camber Sands[1] with stylist Melanie Ward and made a set of pictures with Kate. It was one of those stories where they went back to the location at least three times, an approach I would encourage with a lot of photographers at the time, as we worked to build stories together. The final images that ran captured Kate's teen spirit. But while it looked like she was wearing her own clothes, she's totally styled, actually wearing a lot of things Melanie and Corinne would wear at the time. They basically styled Kate as themselves: Birkenstock shoes, cheesecloth dresses, plus daisies around her neck. Kate wasn't a hippy-trippy chick. She was a streetwise Croydon girl who I'd see out at clubs. But even styled in this manner, her natural personality came through. The one really important thing relating to this was that there was very, very little fashion advertising in *The Face*. So we didn't have to adhere to that policy of putting certain clothing on somebody because there was an advertising page later in the magazine. We didn't have that restriction and that enabled people to feel more like themselves, which was great.

NICK LOGAN:

I remember liking the image, but it still wasn't that common for us to use a fashion image for a cover story. Sheryl said, "I've got these stories which I could pull together for the third summer of love." I said, "Brilliant, let's go with it." So it was pure accident, digging ourselves out of a hole.

SHERYL GARRATT:

Phil deserves the credit – not me. My memory was that we were hoping to get a shot from Spike Island[2] for the cover but couldn't get one, so we were casting about for something else. Phil came up with the shot of Kate. I didn't think it worked. Nick suggested we did Sandra Bernhardt who was a Q&A on the back page. We tried a Herb Ritts shot of her but it didn't work. It was too Eighties. Then Phil cut the feathers out from the headdress and put it over the masthead. Suddenly, it felt very forward-looking. It went from flat to cheeky, irreverent.

I didn't want any more of that pouting thing in fashion in the Eighties, that inaccessible perfection. I wanted more joy and colour because that's what was happening in dance and pop culture at the time. Everything had gone technicolour.

PHIL BICKER:

It had been a summer of festivals and ecstasy and it seemed that the Kate pictures had all those qualities without it being so literal. That was exactly what I wanted.

No one remembers it now, but we had done a Kate cover in May.[3] It was a World Cup cover and it was forgettable at best: it didn't feel like Kate at all. We'd only ever had a couple of people appear on the cover twice – one was Madonna – so why would we put this 16-year-old girl from Croydon on the cover two months later? There was a lot of kickback in the office about it.

I give credit to Nick for having his wits about him to see what was there. It wasn't an obvious cover but it was positive, spirited and natural. Its vibrancy was the opposite in a way to the stoic Felix on the "Killer" cover. It took the editors of *Vogue* another couple of years before they first worked with Kate: the quote was that they were waiting as "she hadn't grown into her features yet". That's what I was trying to beat.

We'd just been through Ray Petri and "Buffalo" which was very stylized fashion. Ray had died the previous year and we were looking for a new direction. Corinne and David Sims, in particular, brought that new kind of grunge, as it was later labelled, with Melanie's styling. Corinne's work with Kate was the beginning of that new look. It was very natural at first but it got dirtier as it went on. Heroin chic was born out of it, but this cover is the antithesis of that.

SHERYL GARRATT:

Corinne was exceptional. The way she shot was almost documentary. When she photographed musicians or actors she wasn't that bothered and would pose them, but when she photographed models she tried to show their personality. I think that was partly because every time she had modelled she felt her personality had been stolen from her.

---

1   Beach in East Sussex, UK.
2   Stone Roses' epic May Bank Holiday gig in Widnes, north-west England, 27 May 1990.
3   Photographed by Mark Lebon.

COLORS

LAUNCH ISSUE, AUTUMN/WINTER 1991

Co-founder of the Benetton group:
    Luciano Benetton
Editorial director: Oliviero Toscani
Editor-in-chief: Tibor Kalman
Cover by Oliviero Toscani & Tibor Kalman

ISSUE 2, SPRING/ SUMMER 1992

Cover credit (on p.2): "Albanians trying to
    flee their country swarm to ships in the
    port of Durres last August; 4,000
    attempted to board the freighter *Vlora*,
    bound for Italy. (We guess no one told
    them what a drag it is to visit Italy in
    August)."
Cover picture: Associated Press
Cover by Oliviero Toscani, Tibor Kalman,
    Karrie Jacobs, Lucy Shulte, Alice Albert

In 1982 Italian photographer Oliviero Toscani joined forces with global fashion brand Benetton to create the decade's most contentious advertising campaign. Called "United Colors of Benetton", it promoted the company's values over their clothes with provocative images that played with multiculturalism and the politics of difference. For their Autumn/Winter 1991 campaign, Toscani decided "to take a photograph that could not be censored. Something that would unite everyone, an untouchable image."[1] The image of a baby girl, Giusy, at the moment of birth, was widely attacked. It also became the launch cover of *Colors*, the new magazine Toscani then developed with trailblazing designer Tibor Kalman.

LUCIANO BENETTON:

A mutual friend, Elio Fiorucci, introduced me to Oliviero 36 years ago. I had been impressed by his Jesus Jeans campaign.[2] I was looking for someone with the ability to develop a non-traditional form of communication. Oliviero had all the right qualities.

Certainly it was a new philosophy, which instead of focusing on the product had elements of social commitment. As we were investing large sums of money it was worthwhile employing these funds for useful purposes. Our highly innovative approach and form of research surprised and, I think, wrong-footed many, including the advertising agencies.

The idea of *Colors* was financed by Benetton but did not address topics related to the company. Instead it was aimed at young creative people across the world – a magazine that thought outside the box, with extraordinary editors. As far as I was concerned, they had carte blanche. The essential point for me was to highlight different cultures and celebrate their diversities. We were aware it was not a magazine for everyone; it was for a very select audience.

Even for me, the photo of the newborn baby was a strong image, but I supported Tibor and Oliviero's decisions at all times. I have great affection for that first cover. It generated an extraordinary level of debate, with a clear division of public opinion. On one side, for example, the British had the billboards taken down the same day they were put up, while the maternity wards of British hospitals continued to request posters of the image for years afterwards.

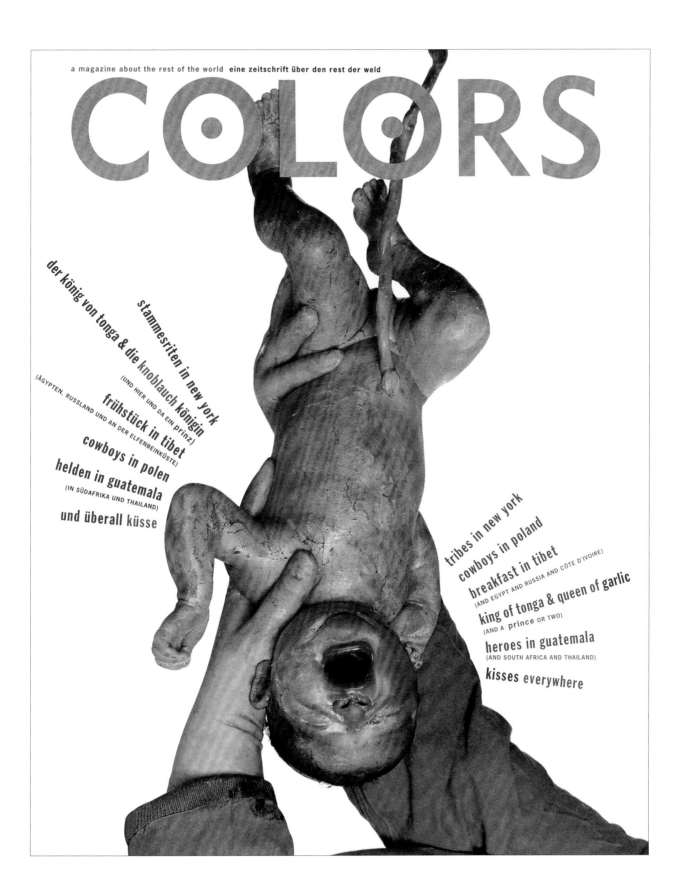

a magazine about the rest of the world **eine zeitschrift über den rest der weld**

COLORS

der könig von tonga & die knoblauch königin
stammesriten in new york
(UND HIER UND DA EIN PRINZ)
frühstück in tibet
(ÄGYPTEN, RUSSLAND UND AN DER ELFENBEINKÜSTE)
cowboys in polen
helden in guatemala
(IN SÜDAFRIKA UND THAILAND)
und überall küsse

BOTSWANA 6.50P CHINA 21Y ESP 430PTA FRANCE 22FF FRG 9,50DM HELLAS 750DR INDIA 70RE ITAL 5.000L JAPAN 600Y MACAO 32P NEDERL 8FL SWITZ 7SFR UK £2.50 USA $4.00 UV 8800A

COLORS

a magazine about the rest of the world no.2 spring summer 1992 ein Magazin über den Rest der Welt nr.2 frühsjahr sommer 1992

IMMIGRATION BRINGS... IMMIGRATION BRINGT... new blood, neues blut, new food, neues essen, new music, neue musik, new words, neue wörter, new movies, neue filme, new beliefs, neue weltanschauungen, new romantic possibilities, neue romantische möglichkeiten, and new excuses for parades, und neue vorwände für paraden ...to an old world. ...IN EINE ALTE WELT.

Television (and other Aphrodisiacs)
Snacks (and other Garbage)
Fake Fat (and other Miracles)
Plus three (3!) Madonnas

Fernsehen (und andere Aphrodisiaka)
Knabberei (und anderer Abfall)
Fettersatz (und andere Wunder)
Plus drei (3!) Madonnen

Moscow goes wild...
Moskau wird wild...

and! the most beautiful chickens in the world
und! die schönsten Hühner der Welt

OLIVIERO TOSCANI:

A lot of the media were not accepting of the Colors campaign. They found it shocking. If you haven't got the balls to face the reality then you will say it is shocking. So I said to Luciano, let's do a magazine with the leftover money. But at the beginning it wasn't easy to sell it, not even to Luciano. As Machiavelli says, there is nothing more difficult and daring and complicated than something that starts a new path.

And, of course, you have to have people with you. After many interviews I chose Tibor. He worked for me. He was an arguer, he was a complainer. But what I really enjoyed about him was that he was intelligent. I always look for somebody who is on the other side of the wind. *Colors* was made with that idea.

I said, "Tibor, I want to do a magazine that doesn't exist, OK?" He was very fashion, very hip. He was working at *Interview* and he knew the places, he knew the people. I didn't want all that. First of all, everybody who comes and works at *Colors* should not have been a journalist before. It had to be their first experience so they will make great mistakes. Second, we had to make a magazine where the words are not serving the images and the images are not serving the words but they have to cross constantly. We have to make a magazine with no news and no celebrities. And more than that: it was in English always with another language. Normally, those two-language magazines are too boring. They look like company magazines but I didn't mind that. Actually, I had major discussions with Tibor about the first issue because he was afraid that *Colors* was too much of a corporate magazine and he didn't believe that a magazine without news and celebrities would work.

A cover has to provoke a reaction. Since marketing took over, provocation is a bad word. We have to eat everything soft, tasteless, chewable, digestible, and we get poison from that. When the first cover came out, the BBC interviewed me and I said, "Oh, of course, you British get upset to see a new-born baby. You wouldn't get shocked if it was a puppy."

The immigration cover is very modern, still today. It wasn't new at the time. That's an issue that goes on forever. There was a lot of immigration from Albania to Italy and suddenly Italy understood that we were a place where immigrants wanted to go. Normally, we were the country that wanted to go somewhere else. We pushed the fact that immigration is an incredibly positive thing. Look at what is written on the cover. Immigration brings new blood, new beliefs, new romantic possibilities – fantastic! You never put together those words. That was the copy I was looking for, to put together image and words to create a new meaning. That's typical *Colors*.

1 Quoted in Lorella Pagnucco Salvemini, *United Colors*, Scriptum Editions, 2002, p.50.

2 Controversial 1971 ad campaign by Toscani and Emanuele Pirella which superimposed Christ's pronouncement, *"Chi mi ama, mi segua"* ("If you love me, follow me") on a female bottom in denim mini-shorts.

VANITY FAIR

AUGUST 1991
Editor-in-chief: Tina Brown
Art and design director: Charles Churchward
Cover photographer: Annie Leibovitz
Stylist: Lori Goldstein
Features editor: Jane Sarkin

Tina Brown had been looking for a cover that "moved *Vanity Fair* decisively on from the 1980s, that made a statement of modernity, progressiveness, freshness, openness, after the heavy Trumpy glitz of that decade".[1] This was it.

During the session, Leibovitz had done a full-body nude shot privately for Moore, who was seven months pregnant with her second daughter, Scout LaRue. Moore recalls that during the shoot, "I commented that it would be great if they would use this for the cover, never giving it a second thought because I didn't imagine they'd be brave enough to use it."[2] Leibovitz agreed it would make a great cover: "Before then, if you were pregnant, you were supposed to hide in the corner and be heavily clothed."[3] After some lively debate at the magazine, Brown said a hugely enthusiastic yes and Moore also gave her approval. Condé Nast knew that there would be an uproar, so they warned the news trade in advance. Some refused to sell it; some demanded it be hidden in a wrapper like a pornographic magazine, making it even more tempting.

There was a media feeding frenzy. The arguments raged: it liberated pregnancy; it championed female empowerment; it was a powerful feminist statement; it screamed sexual objectification; it was high art; it was obscene. Brown added: "It seems we have broken the last taboo. And the perfection of it was that it was an unassailable platform for controversy. Who's ever managed to shock with family values before?"[4] Moore agreed, later commenting: "I did feel glamorous, beautiful and more free about my body. I don't know how much more family-oriented I could possibly have gotten."[5]

Sales went from 800,000 to well over a million. Its influence was enormous. Rival magazines plundered the idea.[6] It added further fuel to the tabloids' obsession with baby bumps and was even "held responsible for the rise of body-hugging maternity fashion".[7]

VANITY FAIR

AUGUST 1991/$2.50

More Demi Moore

by Nancy Collins

DARYL GATES
Is L.A.'s Top Cop
to Blame?
by Fredric Dannen

**HOW SADDAM
SURVIVED**
by Gail Sheehy

**SHOWDOWN
AT THE
BARNES COLLECTION**
by John Richardson
and David D'Arcy

VÁCLAV HAVEL
Philosopher King
by Stephen Schiff

**HOLLYWOOD
MAYHEM**
What Is
Joe Eszterhas's
Basic Instinct?
by Lynn Hirschberg

CHARLES CHURCHWARD:

We didn't know what we were going to get with someone that pregnant, but Annie knew Demi was one of those people you could collaborate with on extreme shots, something you didn't often find with actors at that time.

The naked shot wasn't specifically planned. The back-up was a close-up head portrait. Some clothes were sent out and I don't think we were even sure that we could use them. Lori Goldstein is important. She has that special talent of understanding what a photograph needs, how things can change in two seconds and you have to come up with a whole different outfit. The one difference between then and now – and it changed soon after this picture, really – is that fashion advertisers began insisting on their clothes being used, influencing covers. It became more difficult for stylists who brought what was best for the photo.

I believe Lori brought the green satin Isaac Mizrahi robe you see inside for the cover. It was for the colour and the fact you can do almost anything with it. Also, the diamond earrings[8] – in case nothing else works, at least you've got some shiny earrings.

The pictures came in and they caused quite a stir. The staff argued for days, back and forth. I laid out covers all different ways; one of them must have been the Mizrahi robe. The staff was fighting over the nude shot so much that it seemed like a good idea to put it on the cover. We knew something was there but we didn't know how much and what the reaction was going to be. From the first day, it became one of those covers that everybody was talking about, making magazine history.

1   Tina Brown, *The Vanity Fair Diaries, 1983–1992*, Weidenfeld & Nicolson, 2017, p.400.

2   Demi Moore in interview with Ian Birch.

3   Joanna Robinson, "Annie Leibovitz Speaks for the First Time About Her Historic Caitlyn Jenner Cover", *Vanity Fair*, 6 October 2015.

4   Tina Brown, *The Vanity Fair Diaries, 1983–1992*, Weidenfeld & Nicolson, 2017, p.400.

5   Quoted in Maxine Mesinger, "VF Dresses Demi in Paint", *Houston Chronicle*, 7 July 1992.

6   For example, *W*, *German Vogue*, American *Harper's Bazaar* and Australian *Marie Claire*.

7   Annie Liebovitz, *Annie Liebovitz At Work*, Jonathan Cape London, 2008, p.91.

8   The diamond jewellery was by Laykin et Cie.

ESQUIRE

FEBRUARY 1992

Editor-in-chief: Terry McDonell
Art director: Rhonda Rubinstein
Design consultant: Roger Black

This was the cover that brought back the bite that the American *Esquire* brand had in the 1960s.[1]

TERRY MCDONELL:

I'd always thought that there was a wealth of telling imagery around white culture, but that few people noticed because they saw it all the time. In some cases it seemed grotesque to me, and in others sort of sweet.

We got these great pictures that were emblematic of white culture in America and ran them inside. One of my favorites was of a white breakfast at a Howard Johnson's,[2] exactly the kind of thing you pass over depending on how immersed you are in that culture. I'm talking about the white pancakes, the white placemat, the white milk. It was hilarious.

At the same time, I was working with Richard Ben Cramer on a story about the first Bush presidency called "George Bush's White Men". Richard was reporting for his seminal book *What It Takes: The Way to the White House*[3] and he had detail after detail that echoed the pictures with a subtext that asked "Is America really racist or not?"

To illustrate the piece, we used a photo of Bush in his living room in Kennebunkport, with lots of chintz and a horrible painting of children with big eyes by Margaret Keane. Bush is dressed casually and all his advisors are sitting around in white shirts. These are very, very white guys. Bush was unpopular at that time because of the Gulf War. It was a heightened political moment.

I wanted the cover to be as graphic as possible and that meant going with type. That would be surprising, and when you're surprising, readers pay attention. It was meant to be political, of course, and ironic because *Esquire* had a white readership. In that sense, the cover had a wonderful biting-the-hand-that-feeds-you feel to it.

RHONDA RUBINSTEIN:

The pictures we ran inside were ironic images by photographers such as Elliott Erwitt and Stephen Shore which poked fun at the lifestyles of gun-toting, flag-waving true believers — decades before the dubious achievement of "Make America Great Again". These documentary photos would not make for a great iconic cover, though we did try various comps.

The all-type cover emerged from Terry's fascination with the almost-imageless *Granta* cover on the family[4] and Roger Black's admiration of the Beatles' White Album. The simplicity and strength of the huge sans serif WHITE PEOPLE — filling the cover as large as possible, but still almost invisible – was further mocked by its 9-point small-cap subtitle. Due to the nuanced nature of this white-on-white design, execution was paramount. That happened during a long night on press when we enhanced the whiteness of WHITE PEOPLE by coating it with a clear glossy varnish.

TERRY MCDONELL:

Some people thought it was a mistake. There was a lot of "This is the one that's going to get you fired". Maybe it did. My editors thought it was very cool. Hearst management didn't quite understand it the same way, for obvious reasons.

All the best covers have an element of humour, and the humour here is the line at the bottom, "The Trouble with America". It's a kind of inside joke that the readership would get and identify with. It's tribal: we are smart together, we laugh at the same jokes. Like Bill Buford's cover of *Granta* about "The Family", which had a photograph of an idyllic *Father Knows Best*-like mom and dad and kids[5] with the line "They Fuck You Up". I thought it was wonderful, inspiring.

So I really wanted to do that White People cover. Did it sell? Not so much.

---

1 *See* page 27.
2 US hotel and restaurant chain.
3 Published by Random House in 1992, Richard Ben Cramer's book is regarded as a seminal account of the 1988 presidental election.
4 *Granta* 37, 1 October 1991.
5 A reference to a popular US radio and television sitcom of the 1950s.

esquire

THE MAGAZINE FOR MEN

FEBRUARY 1992·$2.50

WHITE PEOPLE

THE TROUBLE WITH AMERICA

ROLLING STONE

20 AUGUST 1992
Editor and publisher: Jann S Wenner
Art director: Fred Woodward
Photographer: Mark Seliger
Photography director: Laurie Kratochvil
Grooming: Lori Matsushima/Cloutier
Styling: Arianne Phillips/Visage
Cover story by Alan Light

In June 1992 a Texas Law Enforcement Association called CLEAT became aware of the words in "Cop Killer" by Ice-T's speed metal band, Body Count. They were outraged by lines like "I'm 'bout to bust some shots off / I'm 'bout to dust some cops off" and called for a boycott of Time Warner, the record's distributor. The controversy escalated, with high-profile figures such as President George Bush and Vice President Dan Quayle condemning the lyrics.

Ice-T, who wrote the words, defended it as a protest against police brutality: "It's a record about a character. I know the character, I've woken up feeling like this character."[1] All this was happening only two months after Los Angeles had witnessed six days of civil disturbance unleashed by the acquittal of four LAPD officers accused of using excessive force in the arrest of Rodney King.

Mark Seliger suggested putting him in full police uniform for the cover. Ice-T remembers Seliger saying, "This is the ultimate nightmare of a racist cop ... getting pulled over by you and having you have the billy club. It actually did what he said it was going to. It outraged a lot of people."[2] Fred Woodward brilliantly highlighted the tension in the fractured black-and-white typography.

ALAN LIGHT:

Mark and I had dinner the night before and he laid out the idea to me and we talked about whether Ice would go for it. I felt that he would get it, that he was savvy and brave enough to understand the kind of statement the uniform would make. It was provocative, no doubt, but that has always been Ice's game – and it was smart, it wasn't just provocative for its own sake.

MARK SELIGER:

I was working with Arianne, who is all about precision and accuracy.[3] Without her attention to detail – the baton, the cap, the badge, the carefully fitted shirt – the picture wouldn't have had the same kind of emotion.

We decided we wanted a very simple, stripped-out background. I didn't want there to be anything too distracting. We didn't tell Ice-T the idea until he got

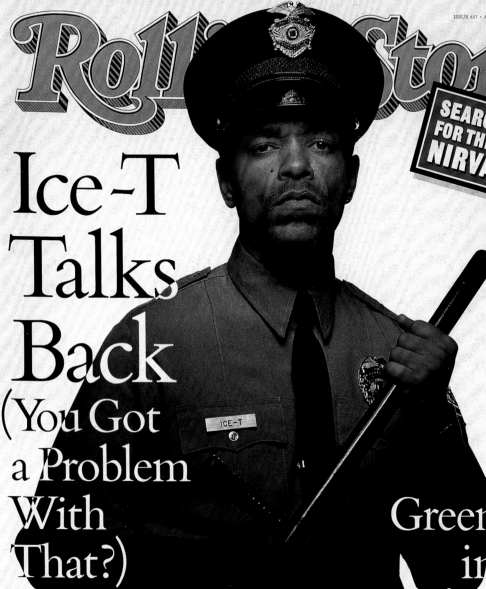

Rolling Stone

ISSUE 637 · AUGUST 20TH, 1992 · $2.50 · CAN $2.95

SEARCHING
FOR THE NEW
NIRVANA

Ice-T
Talks
Back
(You Got
a Problem
With
That?)

ICE-T

Greenmail
in Rio:
P.J. O'Rourke
at the Earth
Summit

34
34790
0 140235 3

there. He walked in and I said, "Want to have some fun?" He was a really warm, lovely guy, not an aloof artist, but very focused, and wanted to know your ideas.

I showed him the cop outfit and he goes, "I'm in," without any hesitation. When he stepped into the uniform, he became the character. He's also an actor, so it was a natural experience for him.

ARIANNE PHILLIPS:

He owned it. He understood the gravitas of how powerful the message would be on the cover of *Rolling Stone*.

MARK SELIGER:

I tried to create a kind of a poignant moment through the lighting. I wanted it to silhouette and the white background really helped that. We used a small light source to make everything drop off. I didn't want the gun to be a main focus. It's a movie gun, of course. We wouldn't bring a real gun to the set. The baton sold you on the idea that, even if they're not pointing a gun on you, they could beat you up.

It was important for me to have an understanding of what Ice-T was saying, so I asked him, "Do you really want to kill cops?" He said, "Look, do people question Bob Dylan when he writes a song about revolution or injustice or how the police and government mishandle power? No."

He likened it to writing a script for a John Ford movie. You don't see somebody going up to John Ford after a sheriff gets murdered in one of his Westerns and calling him a sheriff killer.

Once I'm done, I move on the next photograph. I typically don't follow what the reaction is, but Laurie sent me a handwritten note when she got the image, saying your pictures of Ice-T are absolutely amazing – make sure you duck when the shit hits the fan.

ALAN LIGHT:

Remember that Ice-T had already played a cop in the *New Jack City* movie. As he said in the "Cop Killer" interview, no one pinned a medal on him for presenting an upstanding cop, then they went crazy when he talked about a character wanting revenge on a bad cop.

No doubt the image upset a lot of people. But the thing about Ice-T is that he was up to any intellectual challenge and he knew (and we knew) that he could explain it, answer for it, back it up no matter what debate he might face. That was the secret weapon – he is so good that he didn't need to fear having to explain his decisions, and that's what people weren't ready for.

1 Ice-T to Alan Light, "The Rolling Stone Interview", *Rolling Stone*, 20 August 1992, p.31.
2 *Rolling Stone: Stories from the Edge*, documentary (dir. Alex Gibney and Blair Foster), Sky Arts, November 2017.
3 Arianne Philipps subsequently became a celebrated costume designer and Madonna's stylist for many years. She has been nominated for two Oscars.

HARPER'S BAZAAR

RELAUNCH ISSUE, SEPTEMBER 1992

Editor-in-chief: Elizabeth (Liz) Tilberis

Creative director: Fabien Baron

Cover model: Linda Evangelista

Cover photography: Patrick Demarchelier

Terry McDonell was editor-in-chief of
    Hearst's *Esquire* (1990–3).[1]

In 1992 Hearst lured Liz Tilberis away from British *Vogue* to American *Harper's Bazaar*. Her goal was to make *Bazaar* the most beautiful fashion magazine in the world. And, for a time, she did. She recruited a dream team including Fabien Baron, whose previous work at *New York Woman,* Italian *Vogue* under Franca Sozzani and *Interview* had marked him out as a major international talent. Baron transformed the tired title, reconnecting it to the ground-breaking art direction of Alexey Brodovitch between 1934 and 1958. This was the relaunch issue. *Vogue* took notice: it now had serious competition.

TERRY MCDONELL:

Vogue was going downtown, flirting with grunge. Liz went the opposite direction, cool but without any snobby chill. Fabien was the perfect collaborator. His typography was relentlessly innovative and sophisticated. Just look at the way he unbalanced the logo. Totally modern. By comparison, *Vogue*'s grunged-up models covered with type looked sloppy.

FABIEN BARON:

We felt the time was right for a radical change. We all wanted to do something really memorable, and Liz was ready to push for something new all the way to the cover. Magazine covers were quite busy in those days, covered in type, with complicated pictures, so I felt going simple and direct was the way to go. I liked the idea of a model playing with the logo, maybe tilt a letter to give the idea that *Bazaar* was changing.[2]

It was also her look – Linda's hair, attitude, and the fact that it was shot on a white background with just a single headline, and that Linda was the number-one model at the time. I said to Liz, "Let's make a statement, let's make it clear that it's new." It also came exactly at the time when the fashion message was shifting. Grunge and a new realness were starting, but we were also embracing elegance in a new way. That is what made *Bazaar* so special at the time – that mix of high and low, executed to the nth degree. Everything was controlled, perfected, and finished in a way other magazines had never gone before. You have to remember that when we took the magazine over, *Bazaar* was about "looking good at 40". This cover said, "to hell with all that stuff". It was a breath of fresh air and it became the magazine of reference for the fashion industry.

Bazaar became the perfect competition to *Vogue*. We didn't do it to give Anna [Wintour] a rough time; we just wanted to say something else and there was room to do that. Being more creative and forward was our goal, but that definitely created a war between Condé Nast and us at Hearst. Everybody out there thought we were doing the right thing though.

Liz was an amazing editor and the team visionary. We all loved her, and she understood how to work with people in a way that let them do what they did best.

---

1 McDonell had a pact with Tilberis: she would help him with *Esquire*'s fashion; he would help her with "getting on in America".

2 It was also a reference to the December 1959 cover art directed by Henry Wolf featuring a Richard Avedon photograph of the American model Dovima climbing a ladder while carrying the letter "A".

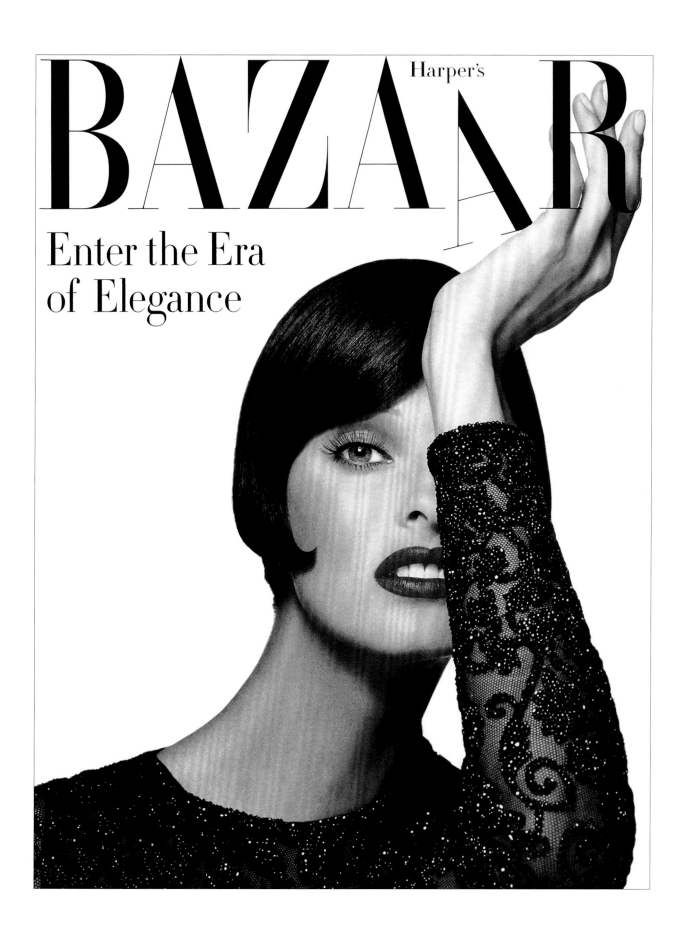

BAZAAR

Harper's

Enter the Era
of Elegance

WIRED

LAUNCH ISSUE, JANUARY 1993

President: Jane Metcalfe

Editor-in-chief/publisher: Louis Rossetto

Executive editor: Kevin Kelly

Creative directors:

   John Plunkett & Barbara Kuhr

Cover photography: Neil Selkirk

Former novelist and tech evangelist Louis Rossetto wanted a new kind of magazine that fused 1960s hippie radicalism and libertarianism with his fervent belief in the power of the new digital technology to transform society for the better. He and his partner, Jane Metcalfe, teamed with designers John Plunkett and Barbara Kuhr in 1987 to develop a *Rolling Stone* for the digital age.

JOHN PLUNKETT:

We had high goals, philosophically and creatively. Louis and I had read two books: Stewart Brand's *The Media Lab: Inventing the Future at M.I.T.* and William Gibson's debut novel, *Neuromancer*. If you combine them, you can sort of see the germination of the magazine.

The design was not just me, but also my partner, Barbara Kuhr. When you're going from an old medium to a new one, you have a Catch-22. You have to use the old medium to announce the new one, so it's like the telegraph saying that the telephone is coming. Or ink on paper to announce electrons.

I wanted the cover and front sections to feel like lit-up screens, with text and images that flowed horizontally rather than up and down. I wanted it to look like you were walking into the middle of a conversation. That's what the dot-to-dot ellipsis design is meant to signify: "The Medium…" cover line. McLuhan was a big influence, so for the first issue we used his quote, which happens to be the first sentence of the first paragraph of *The Medium is the Massage*.[1] It's an amazing statement which is still becoming true, and somehow this man wrote it in 1967.

Louis made the great decision to put a writer, Bruce Sterling,[2] on the first cover. This brought up a whole host of challenges. We were trying to focus on the people who were doing extraordinary things. Not on the technology. But it turned out that most of these people were fairly ordinary looking. Bruce was a slightly overweight, mild-mannered, middle-aged white guy. He came in with a suit and tie, but we wanted to make him look as amazing as his work.

I had talked a lot with Neil, the photographer, prior to Bruce's arrival, about what can we do through technique to create an image that's not perfect, that is disjointed, just intermediated in some way. And Neil came up with a very simple device. It was literally some mirrored tiles that you would put on a bathroom wall. But if you fold those over a chair and then photograph someone's reflection in that, it creates the illusion of a "digitized" image.

NEIL SELKIRK:

They were one-inch-square mirrored tiles glued to a fabric so that they can follow a contour. Essentially, you just move the camera backwards and forwards until the person starts looking interesting. It also had the effect of looking pixellated. It was a considered solution to a problem rather than a piece of highly imaginative image making.

JOHN PLUNKETT:

It occurred to me, if we came in close on his eyes, we could say this guy had seen the future of warfare. It was a great story about cyber warfare.

Louis, Kevin and I really did see ourselves as a sort of pirate ship. We shared a belief that – and it differentiated us from most journalists – one should choose to be optimistic. It was a sort of militant optimism despite the best evidence. The magazine was an expression of that.

---

1 McLuhan's quote continues over the first five editorial pages with horizontal typography by Plunkett, and a "digitized" collage of images collected by him and illustrator Eric Adigard.

2 American science fiction writer whose work helped shape cyberpunk literature.

RAYGUN

JUNE/JULY 1994

Founder, editor-in-chief & publisher:
Marvin Scott Jarrett

Founder & executive publisher:
Jaclynn B Jarrett

Art direction & design: David Carson

Executive editor: Randy Bookasta

Cover: "Music and Animals" – three images
combined in Photoshop and as collage

Photograph of Perry Farrell:
Melodie McDaniel

Photograph of plane: Dan Conway

Photograph of dog: Jason Lamotte

Taking its name from David Bowie's song "Moonage Daydream",[1] the music monthly emerged in late 1992 at "the height of grunge, the early stages of electronica, and an important time in the development of indie rock", remembers Randy Bookasta.[2] The magazine's look was even more alt. David Carson, top-ranked surfer-turned-designer, unspooled one design convention after another, creating an interface of exuberant drift and decay, a sort of controlled chaos, in stark contrast to newsstand rivals *Spin* and *Rolling Stone*.

MARVIN SCOTT JARRETT:

My idea was to create an alternative music and design magazine that was as disruptive in the print world as MTV had been in television. I loved David Carson's work at *Beach Culture*[3] and thought by bringing him into a music magazine it could be revolutionary.

DAVID CARSON:

I tried never to repeat myself, and don't believe I did. You won't find two covers that look the same, in any respect. I hope all my work, as David Byrne described it, communicates "on a level beyond words ... and goes straight to the part that understands without thinking".[4] The Perry Farrell cover is largely me trying to experiment with layering and things that had become possible with Photoshop, even though I didn't myself use it. It combined some press photos with a portfolio piece someone had sent me. I was trying to use more colour than I normally did. I like the script font I would never have used, and haven't since. I think it kind of fits. I'm using the cover as my canvas, painting with shapes and letters and photos. I like that you can discover things in it and, in its own way, I think it fits the artist and music. What did Perry think of it? I never heard. I rarely did.

RANDY BOOKASTA:

This was a beautiful cover and a great example of David Carson's design taking multiple assets he was provided by our contributors to another level – the cover photo of Perry, illustrations, original fonts. One of our favourite photographers, Melodie McDaniel, took the image of Perry, and she also shot the photos of Trent Reznor inside. Carson actually intertwined both features inside the magazine to unique effect.

1 "Put your ray gun to my head".
2 Email interview with Ian Birch.
3 *Beach Culture* produced only six issues between 1989 and 1991 but won more than 150 design awards for Carson's art direction. In many ways, it was a spawning ground for *Raygun*.
4 David Byrne, 'Introduction', in Lewis Blackwell, *The End of Print: The Grafik Design of David Carson*, Laurence King, 2000.

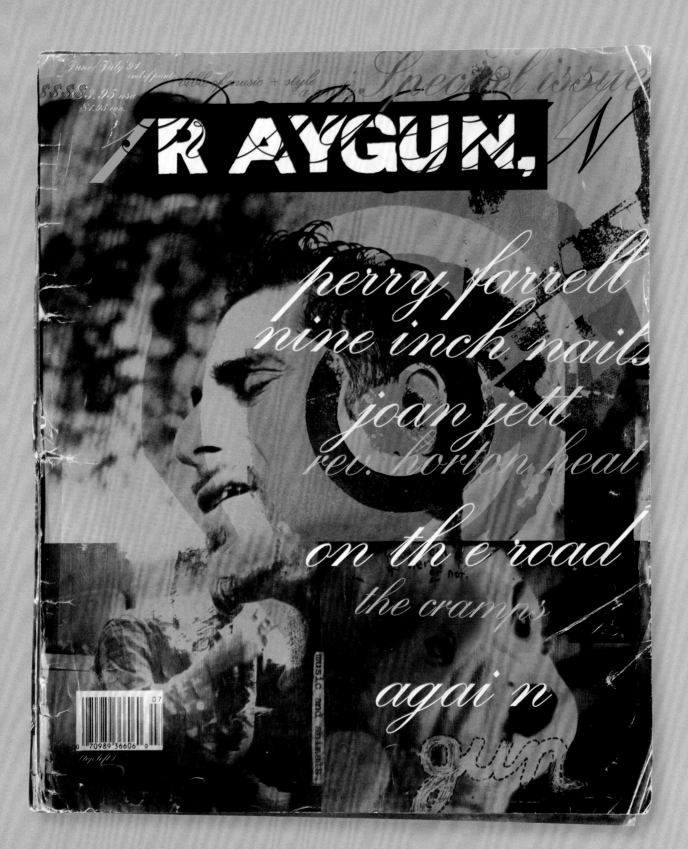

June/July '94 end of print bill music + style Special Issue
$$$$3.95 usa
$4.95 can.

R AYGUN,

perry farrell
nine inch nails
joan jett
rev. horton heat

on th e road
the cramps

agai n

THE ECONOMIST

10–16 SEPTEMBER 1994
Editor-in-chief: Bill Emmott
Head of graphics: Penny Garrett
Head of picture desk: Celina Dunlop

The Economist has a long and noble history of irreverent covers: this image of "coital camels" was especially notorious. The cover story warned of the dangers lurking in the $210 billion worth of corporate mergers that had been announced so far that year.

BILL EMMOTT:

We may look as if we are part of the establishment, being a kind of high politics and business magazine read by relatively well-off people, but actually we like to stick two fingers up to the establishment on every possible relevant and appropriate occasion.

The camel cover was a strongly held and well-researched piece on the great temptation in business to "go for the deal" which makes the immediate bosses feel strong and proud, but which is not necessarily very good for the company, the shareholders or indeed the employees. I'm sure we could do the same thing now.

CELINA DUNLOP:

We were all sitting in Bill's office. The cover story had been agreed. We pretty quickly got the cover line. Honestly, a vision then just popped into my head, and that's quite troubling when you think it was animals mating.

We look for humour in everything. So it didn't feel like a sackable offence to say to Bill and everyone in the meeting, I see a rather ungainly coupling of ungainly animals – the idea that two companies would awkwardly approach each other and awkwardly merge. To my relief, everyone laughed.

Then it was about finding something that was acceptable because with some animals there's too much on show. We went through hundreds of pictures

The Economist

SEPTEMBER 10TH-16TH 1994

The trouble with mergers

US$3.50•C$4.50•MPeso 17.50

Australia	A$6.50	China	RMB 40	Hong Kong	HK$35
Bahrain	Dinar 3.5	France	FFr25	India	Rs70
Canada	C$4.50	Germany	Dm7.50	Italy	Lire 7,000

Japan	¥850(本体825)	Russia	US$3.50	Switzerland	SFr7.50
Mexico	Peso17.50	Saudi Arabia	Rials 25	UK	£2.00
Netherlands	FL8.50	South Africa	Rand 15.50	USA	$3.50

0 09281 02674 7

of animals copulating. We ended up with camels because they were nicely discreet. They could almost be hugging each other.

BILL EMMOTT:

It went out on the Thursday night and I must admit I suddenly thought, "I wonder how this will go down." Being the way time zones work, the first message I got came from Singapore. I remember thinking, "Uh-oh, Lee Kuan Yew[1] will be giving me a caning for this." But it was from a reader there saying it was the funniest thing that they'd seen in a long time. So I got an immediate lift from a surprising source.

As we went around the world, the most divided view we got was from America, where some people thought it was absolutely hilarious and others thought it was disgusting, blasphemous – well, not *blasphemous* but impure, if you like, and generally beneath the dignity of a supposedly serious magazine. A sort of "Outraged of Louisville, Kentucky".

CELINA DUNLOP:

We had a massive postbag. The response was completely 50/50. There were the "antis" who said, "I couldn't leave this out in front of my children or my clients." One of my favourites was, "The female camel is obviously in pain." The self-appointed feminists said, "How can you possibly depict this ravishment of a female camel?" I wrote back, "I'm not expert enough to know if that's a look of bliss or pain." On the other hand, other people said, "Can I have 14 copies because I want to give it to all my clients."

---

1   The first prime minister of Singapore. In 1994 he was "Senior Minister".

WALLPAPER*

**LAUNCH ISSUE, SEPTEMBER/
OCTOBER 1996**

Editor-in-chief: Tyler Brûlé
Art director: Herbert Winkler
Photographer: Stewart Shining
Fashion stylist: Anne-Marie Curtis
Prop stylist: Michael Reynolds
Tony Chambers joined Wallpaper* as creative
    director in 2003, editor-in-chief in 2007
    and then brand and content director in 2017.

In March 1994 Tyler Brûlé, a Canadian journalist based in the UK, was investigating a story in Afghanistan when he was shot in a sniper attack. While recovering from surgery back in London he hit on the idea for *Wallpaper** and launched it two years later. He gave voice to a style-savvy and entrepreneurial tribe he called "global nomads". *Wallpaper** became a gathering place for a new kind of cool that combined fashion, interiors and travel.

STEWART SHINING:

Tyler described [*Wallpaper**] as a kind of marriage between those independent British magazines like *The Face* and *i-D*, which we grew up on, and traditional American magazines like *Vogue* and *Bazaar*, which were the gold standard. Tom Ford had just come in with Gucci, and that was a big visual moment across the board, fashion-wise and design-wise.[1] That's why the models are in Gucci.

ANNE-MARIE CURTIS:

The dress was photographed without the belt because it didn't arrive. I am one of the few people who know that. I thought, "Is Gucci going to be upset?" but they loved it.

STEWART SHINING:

I, or my agent, asked what the budget was. In those days, that was less an issue. People just had lots of money. Tyler said, "Here's the hitch. We don't really have much money." So we had to do it on a nickel and a prayer. Tyler and Anne-Marie came to New York for the shoot. I'd never seen people so resourceful.

ANNE-MARIE CURTIS:

There was a lot of hustling behind the scenes. There definitely was this duality between how we were doing it and the world we were presenting.

TYLER BRÛLÉ:

When you look back at that cover, in a way it's provocative. We wanted to say this is a magazine that reflected the urbanization we were seeing. The 1970s and 1980s had been about this great flight to the suburbs and we saw the hollowing out of cities in Australia and Europe and North America. This was for people who wanted to be back in town. We wanted to say that in a way that was slick and modern and had a slight nod to the core audience who were born in the early 1970s. There was this world of shelter magazines out there, like *World of Interiors* and *Elle Decoration*, but this had to say fashion as well. And we wanted to speak to a dual audience. Guys should be included.

Culture went to some very dark places then, like heroin chic, but we always wanted to be that constant on the horizon which was sunny and positive and our own place.

TONY CHAMBERS:

It was a brilliant concept – the conflation of fashion and lifestyle, architecture and design. That's what made it sexy. It was ahead of its time then but now is completely mainstream.

1 Gucci, under new creative director Tom Ford, had seen a 90 per cent sales increase between 1995 and 1996.

wall*paper*

*The stuff that surrounds you

sept | oct 1996

launch issue

urban Modernists

£3.00 UK

ISSN 1364-4475

interiors ✳ entertaining ✳ travel

PRIVATE EYE

5 SEPTEMBER 1997

Editor: Ian Hislop

"The Diana cover was extremely controversial, to put it mildly."[1]

IAN HISLOP:

I wanted to suggest that there was an hypocrisy on the part of all of us in our attitude to her. We had consumed photographs, stories, information about her and, at the moment of her death, not only a lot of journalists but also a lot of the general public did an enormous volte-face and turned her into a saint. They started policing other people's levels of grief and were saying, "Well, how bad do you feel? You should feel much worse." They decided that the media were to blame again before they knew whether they were or not.

Then the issue was withdrawn. WH Smith decided they weren't going to sell it. It was in bad taste – which was not their call. Legal issues are bad enough but the magazine largely disappeared.[2] A lot of people just didn't want to sell it. We had to fight to get it back on sale.

We've never had such vitriol from people. They said, "You scumbags, why don't you crawl back under a rock and die?" "You should be strung up." "You are all utterly callous, emotionally crippled public-school twats." You know, fill in the description.

It was one of those periodic outbursts of hysteria, and it made no sense. Francis Wheen, who's the *Eye*'s most brilliant analyst, wrote a piece that morning called "The Mourning Papers" about what Fleet Street had been saying about Diana the week before. Things like "What is this woman doing? Nothing. Wasting her time in a bikini with some Arab playboy in the Mediterranean" and "Doesn't even look after her kids, they're at boarding school all of the time". A week later, she was Mother Teresa. It was a staggering bit of bullshit on the part of the media. They were either in symbiosis with the public or they were following the public, but we didn't join in.

Earl Spencer stood up and berated the surviving parent of two boys whose mother has just been killed saying, "The Windsors are unsuitable to look after you; blood is thicker, etc." He never looked after them at all and he was never going to. They both like their father, and they went and lived with him, unsurprisingly. It was rabble-rousing shite but he got a cheer from outside the funeral. I thought it was a really disgraceful performance by him. It was old-fashioned sort of Tudor aristocratic feuding. He's a shocker.

The royal family were in real trouble. They'd misjudged the mood to start with, they played it in the way they do, aloof and indifferent, trying to carry on as normal, and that wasn't working. But the funeral – the march – saved them because the most emotional part of the whole thing was two small boys in suits walking behind a coffin. Not weeping. Not singing "Candle in the Wind". But doing what we essentially sort of want upper-class British males to do, which is to survive.

Any regrets? Not at all. I didn't feel we traduced anyone or anyone's memory. Sometimes being the little boy who says "There aren't any clothes on" is quite uncomfortable. But, you know, it's the job.

1 Ian Hislop in interview with Ian Birch.
2 Newsstand sales fell by a third.

BLUE

LAUNCH ISSUE
OCTOBER 1997

Publisher/Editor-in-chief: Amy Schrier
Design consultant: David Carson
Cover photography: Laura Levine

Founded in February 1996 by Amy Schrier, New York-based *blue*[1] was an independent lifestyle bi-monthly aimed at the growing interest in adventure travel, cultural exploration and action sports. "The name," says Schrier, "was intended to invoke the associations of blue sky, blue sea and blue planet."[2] Schrier was joined in July by designer David Carson, who had left *Raygun* in 1995 to start his own studio.

AMY SCHRIER:

Bringing David on as co-founder and creative director was probably the most important strategic move *blue* made because it highlighted how important design was going to be in the identity of the magazine. My attraction to his work was what he had done with surfing, snowboarding and skateboarding magazines[3] where his design conveyed the sense of freedom one experiences while doing the activities on the printed page. I wanted him to bring that sense of freedom to travel. We wanted *blue* to be as iconoclastic in the adventure travel field as *Raygun* was in music.

I interpreted the cover as jumping into the unknown, which is what we were doing and also what we imagined our readers were doing in their own travels. The cover image was actually part of a series. We ran three other Laura Levine images of people jumping in the water as full right-hand pages in the front of the magazine. That in itself was unique.

LAURA LEVINE:

My photograph on the cover as well as the three inside were all self-generated, personal fine art photographs conceived and created by me in 1984, years before I ever showed them to David Carson – or anyone else, for that matter. It was not an assignment, nor a collaboration, nor did the concept for the photo originate with an art director.

I happened to be at Jones Beach to shoot a Cyndi Lauper concert for *The New York Times* later that night. I arrived early to hang out by the pool. I was fascinated watching people of all ages, shapes, and sizes jumping off the diving board in a variety of styles and techniques. I visualized shooting a series of unconventional, surreal, minimalistic photographs capturing the divers/jumpers in flight; unusual compositions created in the camera by cropping out body parts in order to produce mysterious images depicting the subjects as

a journal for the new traveler

blue

premiere issue

$3.95 display until octo-
ber 15, 1997

semi-abstract shapes frozen in mid-air against only sky, with no context or reference point as to up or down and no sense of where they were coming from or headed. Total freedom.

These were not professional athletes but regular New Yorkers. For each of them who dared take the leap, there was that one moment, frozen by my camera in mid-air, when they were flying, just like Superman or Supergirl. I achieved this by carefully composing each image in the viewfinder, anticipating each diver's trajectory, and most importantly, intentionally framing and cropping each airborne subject in the camera at the moment I clicked the shutter. I did not have a motor drive so I only took one frame per person. I took one roll of film – 37 images. I used black-and-white film simply because that's what I usually shot, printed and showed. After developing the film, I was pleased to see that practically every frame succeeded in conveying my artistic intent .

Several years later, while making portfolio rounds in LA, I included the contact sheet when showing my book to David Carson at *Beach Culture* in order to propose doing a swimwear fashion spread shot in a similar style. I showed him the contact sheet to give him an idea of what I had in mind, a template of sorts of my concept. He asked if he could hold on to the contact sheet, and that was that.

Several years after that, Carson asked me to print up several of the frames on the contact sheet as a possible cover for *blue*. The cover became one of my cropped-in-camera photos as a full bleed with minimal type and no manipulation. I was very pleased with it and his hands-off approach in running the image as is, respecting the original concept of the mysterious figure flying through the air and whose head I'd cropped out of the frame in that 250th of a second. He used a lovely simple font for the four letters: b l u e. It ran pretty much as I'd intended it to be seen when I first conceived of and shot it.

DAVID CARSON:

This is one of my all time favorite covers. Pretty gutsy for a new mag, but the photo did all that was needed.

LAURA LEVINE:

In 2005, it was named one of ASME's "Top Forty Magazine Covers of the Last Forty Years". Although I was not recognized for my role as the creator of the image, I'm pleased that the cover was honoured.

Figure 10 *Divers, Jones Beach, NY,* 1984. Photographed by and © Laura Levine.

1 This issue can be viewed online (along with the entire seven-year magazine archive) at www.bluemagazine.com.
2 Amy Schrier in interview with Ian Birch.
3 They were *Transworld Skateboarding*, *Beach Culture* and *Surfer*.

2000s

THE NEW YORK TIMES MAGAZINE

8 JUNE 2000

Editor: Adam Moss
Creative director: Janet Froelich
Director of photography: Kathy Ryan
Cover photography: Christopher Anderson
Cover story: Michael Finkel

In 2000 record numbers of Haitians tried to enter America illegally, usually by boat, first to the Bahamas, and from there to Florida. Writer Michael Finkel and photographer Christopher Anderson wanted to document the voyage and persuaded captain Gilbert Marko to take them on his inadequately equipped vessel. "Our trip, it appeared, had all the makings of a suicide mission."[1]

CHRISTOPHER ANDERSON:

I remember the moment Gilbert loaded up the boat. We were told there was going to be something like 25 people. We started counting and when we get to 46 people, we were like, "Wow ...".

When we finally set sail, there was a ceremony on the top deck: songs, prayers and a chicken was sacrificed. Gilbert came down into the hold where we were hidden and sprinkled perfume water everywhere. There was a little locked cabinet in the hold, and every so often he would spray perfume in there too, say a couple of prayers, and then turn around and say, "Nobody go in there."

It was unbelievably hot in the hold. We were stacked literally on top of each other, knees to our chest. You think flying economy across the Atlantic is uncomfortable ... Everything hurt: you felt nauseous from the smell and the dehydration. But the discomfort was far outweighed by the fear.

Up until this point, I really hadn't taken many pictures. I was trying to be very, very judicious about how and when I chose to make them. The act of photographing is a delicate intrusion. For the cover picture, it was the middle of the night and the water was coming up around our ankles. We realized we were sinking and felt this sheer terror that the end had come. David[2] said to me, "Chris, you better start taking pictures now because we're all going be dead in an hour." And so, sort of mechanically, without thinking about it, I made that picture.

The American Coast Guard picked us up before daybreak. They pulled a Zodiac boat up beside ours to transfer people off. They shouted to Mike and me, "Jump!" We had to know what was in that cabinet, so we dove back down into the boat which was now partially submerged and bust open the lock. Inside, we found a Vodou altar and flags. The Haitians have these embroidered Vodou flags of different spirits. They're quite beautiful. We grabbed them as souvenirs and then jumped down onto the Zodiac boat. I didn't get a picture of the inside of the cabinet. Man, I wish I had.

We were saved but I was in a sheer panic, thinking how can I go back to Kathy? I had only six rolls of film. One of them was the roll that I burned as the boat was sinking. It didn't dawn on me at the time that we didn't need 50 pictures. All we needed were the three pictures that they published.

I have thought about this for a long time: why did I make pictures of that moment when I assumed that we were all going to perish and my pictures would perish with me? There was probably a degree of doing something just to keep me occupied. But there was something more. The act of photographing was about my experience as much as the subject's experience. If there is a sense of terror communicated in that image, it's because that's what I was experiencing.

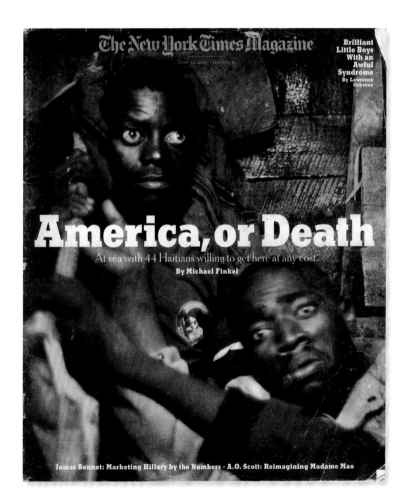

1 Michael Finkel, "Desperate Passage', *The New York Times Magazine*, 18 June 2000.
2 David, a Haitian migrant, acted as their guide and translator. He is bottom right on the cover.

9/11
THE NEW YORK TIMES MAGAZINE

23 SEPTEMBER 2001

Editor: Adam Moss

Art director: Janet Froelich

Photo editor: Kathy Ryan

Cover: "Phantom Towers", conceived by
    Paul Myoda and Julian LaVerdiere; original
    photograph by Fred R Conrad/The New
    York Times; digital manipulation by *The
    New York Times*

On the morning of 11 September 2001 Adam Moss realized that "this is not just an awful event, it's an historical awful event".[1] He asked the team to envision what readers would want to think about nearly two weeks later, when the next issue would come out. He suggested to Janet Froelich that she contact artists and architects for ideas for a memorial, "but most of them", *The New York Times Magazine* then art director remembers, "were too stunned to even consider it."[2] However, artists Paul Myoda and Julian LaVerdiere, who had already been working on an illuminated public sculpture[3] to mount atop the radio tower of World Trade Center 1, suggested "Phantom Towers", the concept that would evolve into the cover of the magazine, and subsequently New York City's annual memorial, "Tribute in Light".

JANET FROELICH:

When we arrived at the magazine that Tuesday morning we thought 30,000 people were dead. We were all grateful that it was one zero less. You had this almost physical pressure on you, the appalling grey dust cloud over Lower Manhattan. I think we all went into a kind of overdrive. You have to rise up out of your own horror and make sense of it on a wider cultural level.

Paul and Julian had been working on a project using beams projected off the top of the building like radio waves. When I went to see them about a memorial, they had this stunning idea of shining two beams up into the heavens from the spot where the Towers had been destroyed, and they sketched it for us (Figure 11).

PAUL MYODA AND JULIAN LAVERDIERE:

We initially did some brainstorming sketches with pencil and paper. We then found an online image of the towers from Jersey City [on the opposite side of the Hudson river], which had been taken after the buildings had come down, and made a version with Photoshop. We simply sculpted that horrific cloud of smoke, which was illuminated because of the rescue effort, into the shape of the Twin Towers. This is when we knew we had the image we wanted. It honestly frightened us because of its strange, ghostly power. At this time we came up with the title of Phantom Towers, because it reminded us of the phenomenon

The New York Times Magazine

SEPTEMBER 23, 2001 / SECTION 6

Remains of the Day By Richard Ford Colson Whitehead Richard Powers Robert Stone James Traub Stephen King Jennifer Egan
Roger Lowenstein Judith Shulevitz Randy Cohen William Safire Andrew Sullivan Jonathan Lethem Michael Lewis Margaret Talbot Charles McGrath
Walter Kirn Deborah Sontag Allan Gurganus Michael Ignatieff Kurt Andersen Jim Dwyer Michael Tolkin Matthew Klam Sandeep Jauhar Lauren Slater
Richard Rhodes Caleb Carr Fred R. Conrad Joju Yasuhide Angel Franco Joel Sternfeld Katie Murray Steve McCurry Carolina Salguero Lisa Kereszi
Jeff Mermelstein William Wendt Andres Serrano Richard Burbridge Paul Myoda Julian LaVerdiere Taryn Simon Kristine Larsen

of the phantom limb – something that is so obviously missing and absent, yet still feels so undeniably present.

JANET FROELICH:

Their project immediately felt like a potential cover. But we had to find a way to make it more than a manipulated skyline photograph. I wanted to convey the mournful quality of the light, the haunting power of the beams. I went through literally hundreds of images of the skyline, but most were lacking that ethereal quality. When I found the Fred Conrad photo (Figure 12), I knew we had the right image. Fred had been on a barge in the Hudson River shooting the wounded area of Lower Manhattan. There was a dust cloud and it was moving, as clouds do, horizontally across the skyline, illuminated perhaps by the moonlight in the cloudless sky.

We brought the image to Nucleus, a digital house we often used, and asked them to make that dust cloud vertical, and to add its reflection in the river. We worked with them for hours to get it right. As the image came together, I knew we had our cover. I phoned my editor, Adam Moss, and he came by to see it. He agreed.

PAUL MYODA AND JULIAN LAVERDIERE:

The image was first posted online, several days before the print version came out. During this time, we saw so many different responses, including many people who tried to politicize the image. Once it became public knowledge that we were working to transition the virtual image into an actual installation, Mayor Rudy Giuliani suggested we make the lights red, white and blue, to represent the firefighters, police and armed forces. We firmly stated we would never agree to this, for the politicization of the Tribute in Light was something we were always strongly against, and stated so publicly whenever we were given the chance. The artistic intent of the project was not to make an American gesture – people from over 90 countries were killed on that day – but rather, we wanted to create beacons of hope for the survivors and beacons of peace for those who perished.

JANET FROELICH:

The Municipal Art Society and Creative Time worked together to make this idea a reality. Every September in the night sky you see it – those twin beams of light shining into the sky from near Ground Zero. It is the most significant news story I was ever privileged to have been involved with.

Figure 11 Paul Myoda and Julian LaVerdiere, Proposal for "Phantom Towers".

Figure 12 Fred Conrad, View of the New York skyline from the Hudson River.

1 Kathy Ryan (ed.), *The New York Times Magazine Photographs*, Aperture Foundation, 2011, p.250.
2 Ibid.
3 It was called the *Bioluminescent Beacon*.

9/11
THE NEW YORKER

24 SEPTEMBER 2001

Editor: David Remnick

Art editor: Françoise Mouly

Cover credit: "9/11/2001" by
   Art Spiegelman & Françoise Mouly

"One of the realities of that day, for myself and for everybody I know, was the blue sky," recalls Françoise Mouly. "It was so difficult because it was such a beautiful day."[1] Mouly and Art Spiegelman had just left their SoHo apartment when they saw the first plane plough into the North Tower. Their immediate instinct was to grab their children from school. Their teenage daughter was at Stuyvesant High School, a few blocks from the Towers. After some difficulty, they found her "and the three of us watched the second tower fall in excruciating slow motion".[2] They turned uptown to get their younger son. Back home, David Remnick had called: he wanted a new cover. Mouly had overseen *The New Yorker*'s covers since 1993, but this one became a wife-and-husband collaboration. It "conveyed something about the abrupt tear in the fabric of reality",[3] she later wrote. It was a tear echoed on the cover, as the North Tower's antenna chops into the "W" of the logo.

FRANÇOISE MOULY:

I had to go into work to do the cover but I didn't want to leave my kids because we were in the part of the city that was quarantined. A friend of mine agreed to stay with them.

I was in complete despair. This was too vast. Nothing seemed adequate. It just seemed so impossible to try to respond to something that was so overwhelming. I said to David the only thing that will work is a black cover, just no cover. He was talking about using a photograph, which would, of course, have had news value because photographs weren't ever used on the cover. Art was not quite as desperate. He was making an image[4] which didn't work and which David hadn't expressed much interest in, but he wasn't giving up on it.

When I told Art that I was considering a black cover, he suggested adding in the two towers, black on black. That made sense to me because it was a double negative, the kind of image that would actually express its own negation. I remember the moment of drawing it and seeing it on the screen and going, "Oh my God, it works." It was difficult to explain why, because it was so subtle, so liminal. It was in between being there and not being there.

We heard on the grapevine that another magazine was considering doing a black cover so we weren't sure for a moment if we could go ahead with ours. But then it was back on.

I was extremely grateful that everybody was willing to go with something as fragile and borderline as this. I hoped readers would not rebel or say, "I don't get it." The image was signed by Art[5] and I remember one reader, who didn't see the black-on-black writing, wrote, "Does Art Spiegelman think he owns black?"

I worked very hard with the pre-press and production people. The guy I worked with a lot, Greg Captain, was stranded in Chicago and, because there were no flights, he had to drive back 14 hours to New York. I couldn't have explained what I was after by phone or email. I showed him the kind of effect I wanted – something that was the essence of fine art like Malevich's *White on White* or Ad Reinhardt's "black" paintings. Without catching up on his sleep, Greg then drove another 12 hours to the plant in Kentucky. They had to be the right blacks.

The image elicited an intense reaction from readers. Scores said they were touched and brought to tears. In many instances, they received the magazine as a subscription. They'd see the black cover, put it down, have breakfast, and, not right away but an hour or two later, the outline of the towers would jump out at them as they were seeing the magazine from a different angle. Then, it was like seeing a ghost.

I made a vow, and it wasn't true for my husband but it was for me and my children, that we wouldn't watch any of the footage on TV. It was breached a year later, on September 11 2002 when my daughter was in the same school and the teacher turned on the TV and made them watch the footage. I thought that was insensitive and cruel.

1   Interview with Ian Birch.
2   Françoise Mouly, *Blown Covers: New Yorker covers you were never meant to see*, Abrams, 2012, p.15.
3   Ibid.
4   Spiegelman's unused image "contrasted the lovely fall weather of that day with the horrible event that happened, with the towers covered in a Christo-like black shroud against a Magritte-style blue sky". Sourced from Jeet Heer, "The Uncredited Collaboration behind The New Yorker's Iconic 9/11 Cover", *The Atlantic*, 11 September 2013.
5   For personal and magazine policy reasons, the cover was originally credited only to Spiegelman. Jeet Heer tells the full story in his article for *The Atlantic* (see note 4).

PRICE $3.50

SEPT. 24, 2001

THE NEW YORKER

9/11
ARENA HOMME+

WITHDRAWN COVER, AUTUMN/WINTER 2001/2002
PUBLISHED COVER, AUTUMN/WINTER 2001/2002

Editor-in-chief & design director:
   Fabien Baron
Fashion editor: Karl Templar
Cover photography: Steven Klein
Editorial director: Ashley Heath

The year 2001 was a big one for boy band *NSYNC, but its star attraction, Justin Timberlake, was itching to head in a more adult R&B direction. Repositioning his image began with the men's fashion bi-annual *Arena Homme+,* which Nick Logan had launched in 1994 as a competitor to *L'Uomo Vogue* and *Vogue Hommes Paris.*

FABIEN BARON:
Repackaging Justin Timberlake? Why not? Justin was at a turning point in his career, and probably at the time of the shoot, if you ask me, already thinking of leaving *NSYNC to go solo. We thought we needed to do something very different from the pretty boy Justin, something much cooler, more dangerous, less expected. At the time I was working a lot with Steven Klein so he was my first choice of photographer. We had already done a very successful shoot together with David Beckham,[1] so it felt like a natural choice and the vibe was a mix of American youth meets suburbia meets sexuality. Justin was really into it, he was very easy to work with.

    After the shoot, when Steven and I looked at the pictures, I thought we should put an American flag in the logo. We were in The Hamptons, at Steven's place, looking at the prints and I said, "Should we burn them and see what happens?" Steven was into it, so we poured gasoline on the prints, set them on fire and quickly put out the flames when we thought it looked interesting. I remember Steven's assistant freaking out. He had spent so much time printing out these final prints we were destroying. We picked one we liked and I thought, "That's really decadent."

The magazine came out exactly on September 11, and that's when I realized the cover was in such poor taste. And the cover line, "Hit Me Baby One More Time", was so wrong. I got on the phone with the president at EMAP, and basically convinced him we should recall the magazine and do a new cover.

I look back at it now, and I still think it was a great cover. We were just unlucky with the timing. Justin was moving from one place to another and that's when the best covers happen.

ASHLEY HEATH:

Steven said to me that it was going to be the rebirth, destruction and resurrection of Justin. He wanted to do something fairly hardcore like a boxer who had been beaten up in the ring. Justin's management knew what they were getting, much as David Beckham's people knew when they came to us. We were very good at reinvention. Beckham was a wow cover at the time and it's almost become a formula now – "Let's take a footballer and make him look a bit homoerotic."

That was a really tough 48 hours. Steven immediately messaged me saying the magazine cannot come out. Fabien felt the same. There was resistance at first from our owners, EMAP, to reprint because of the cost. We didn't have any reserves of the beautiful German 120g gloss paper that we used. Fabien talked very convincingly with senior EMAP management, who said they would reprint. To EMAP's credit, they took the financial hit of at least £100,000. The order was to pulp all the issues. It was such a shame. It was almost like KLF torching £1 million except this was £100,000. I kept a few boxes of issues.

It was reprinted on different stock and the cover had a picture from the same session. It was a nice cover, but I always felt the replacement was like flipping a record and making the B-side the A-side. But the right decision was made.

---

1 The David Beckham in underpants cover, *Arena Homme+*, Autumn/Winter 2000.

HOMME

ARENA+

Justin Timberlake:
Hit Me Baby One More Time
Going Underground
2002 New Fashion Riot

£4.50

9 771353 197013

1 1>

HOMME

ARENA+

Justin Timberlake
Streets Ahead of the Game
Going Underground
2002 New Fashion Spirit
380 Pages of Red Hot Style

4.50

771353 197013

1 2>

ENTERTAINMENT WEEKLY

2 MAY 2003

Managing editor: Rick Tetzeli

Cover photographer: James White

Dixie Chicks (left to right): Emily Robison,
 Natalie Maines, Martie Maguire

Dixie Chicks publicist: Cindi Berger

On 10 March 2003 the Dixie Chicks kicked off their "Top of the World" tour at London's Shepherds Bush Empire. Singer Natalie Maines introduced their song "Travelin' Soldier" with these words: "Just so you know, we're on the good side with y'all. We do not want this war, this violence, and we're ashamed that the President of the United States is from Texas."

Betty Clarke reproduced part of this quote in her review of the concert,[1] which appeared in the *Guardian* two days later. American media outlets pounced and the backlash was ferocious. Right-wing commentators hurled slurs like "Traitors", "the Dixie Sluts" and "Saddam's Angels". The band received death threats. On 20 March 2003 the United States, Britain and several coalition allies invaded Iraq. Two months later Maguire told *Entertainment Weekly*, "We wanted to show the absurdity of the extreme names people have been calling us. How do you look at the three of us and think, those are Saddam's Angels?"[2]

Rick Tetzeli would later say: "At certain times, entertainment can speak to the culture at large, and this cover tapped into the widespread anger over George W Bush's disastrous Iraq adventure. After the Dixie Chicks stated their opposition to that war at a concert in Europe, they were vilified by many – including the US ambassador to Britain – as unpatriotic. The cover image was a ringing endorsement of their right to speak their minds, and in the end, of course, they were proved right: what their president had done was simply tragic."[3]

JAMES WHITE:

The shoot took place in a warehouse in Texas close to where they live and there was no paparazzi around. The first idea was that they would be nude, wrapped around an American flag. But as the shoot began to evolve in preproduction, they wanted to have bumper stickers of the slogans made and put them on their bodies. I thought, "This is not going to look good because they will get wrinkly, and you won't be able to read them clearly."

I really pushed the idea of body paint,[4] which is a laborious process. It takes a long time and you have to figure out exactly where the words are going because there can only be one pose. So, everything had to be mapped out but we got it done really quickly. Within three or four hours everyone had their slogans on.

Cindi Berger, their publicist, was there and they had these intense conversations. The girls had been called a lot of vicious things, and they wanted to show that they weren't OK with this – at all. Every single word was taken seriously in terms of how it could be perceived and what was going to happen if they did write it. All three of them were equally as committed and passionate about doing this.

I definitely thought the cover was going to be controversial, for sure, but the one thing that caught me off guard was how much the photograph was imitated – most of it was tongue-in-cheek, which I like. It was a serious topic and to take it that step further and induce some humour is good.

1 Betty Clarke, "The Dixie Chicks", the *Guardian*, 12 March 2003.

2 Chris Willman, "The Dixie Chicks Take on Their Critics", *Entertainment Weekly*, 2 May 2003.

3 "EW's former editors share their favorite and least favorite covers over the years", *Entertainment Weekly*, 12 October 2015. Reproduced with the kind permission of Rick Tetzeli. http://ew.com/article/2015/10/12/ew-former-editors-favorite-least-favorite-covers/

4 Body painter Tara Meadows was on set as a back-up. Just as well as the shipment of bumper stickers didn't arrive.

THE NEW YORKER

21 JULY 2008

Editor: David Remnick

Art editor: Françoise Mouly

Cover illustration: "The Politics of Fear"
  by Barry Blitt

In the run-up to November 2008's presidential election, Barry Blitt's drawing for the cover for the 21 July issue of *The New Yorker* unleashed an inferno of protest from almost every constituency. Obama campaign spokesman Bill Burton dismissed it as "tasteless and offensive".[1] Republican John McCain thought it "totally inappropriate".[2] There were over 10,000 emails and letters of protest; conservative talk radio was apoplectic. David Remnick quickly responded: "The fact is, it's *not* a satire about Obama – it's a satire about the distortions and misconceptions and prejudices *about* Obama."[3]

Blitt's first sketch (Figure 13) also had Michelle Obama as a Muslim and showed conservative commentators Ann Coulter, Bill O'Reilly and Rush Limbaugh at a window looking horrified "at their 'worst nightmare'". "But it didn't seem correct to attribute the prejudices and hidden fears to only those three pundits, so I asked Barry to refine the image to its essence," Françoise Mouly later explained.[4] Blitt agreed: "It was a purer statement without them."[5]

BARRY BLITT:

I got a thousand emails right away, and that was very unpleasant. I sort of did have an idea that it would create a furore. I had the sketch at home, and a few people I showed it to thought I was crazy. I brought the artwork into *The New Yorker*'s office, which I don't always do, and I walked with Françoise over to the production people. You could see everybody was uncomfortable with it. It seemed like career suicide. David and Françoise were 100 per cent behind it. We all thought it would be immediately understood and that its intent was obvious. It was trying to depict all the innuendo that people were saying, to present how ridiculous it was.

The tide actually turned with *The Daily Show*'s coverage.[6] Before that, it was all hate mail I was getting, and after that I started to get a lot of good email. Either that or the haters got it out of their system right away. Obviously, all of those clips [on *The Daily Show*] were the point of the cover.

FRANÇOISE MOULY:

We were taken to task for not having a caption or a title on the cover to explain it. There was an outpouring of outrage from faithful readers who said, "I understand that you're being ironic. I am sophisticated enough to know that you mean it in jest, but I worry that others will lack that sophistication and will take it literally."

Satire has an object and the problem was that it was not shown here in an obvious way. Because the object of the satire is you, the reader. That's what made people so uncomfortable. Our lack of labelling made it hit home because it's asking, "Are you saying that this is what I am projecting?" The most threatening covers are those that are like mirrors of your prejudice. You see something you recognize.

I'm eternally grateful to David Remnick for having had the *noblesse* to stand up to the opprobrium. I mean, he was called a Nazi by Wolf Blitzer on television but he never offered a retraction or an apology, and now he can be very proud of that. But it wasn't easy at the time to stand by the image. I believe that part of the reason we have been able to publish images that stand the test of time is because they're offered without apologies. If we had to worry that we might have to retract an image, then you don't even try, you know?

Figure 13 Barry Blitt's first drawing for the cover of the 21 July 2008 issue of *The New Yorker*.

1 Sourced from http://www.nbcnews.com/id/25673296/ns/politics-decision_08/t/magazines-satirical-cover-stirs-controversy/#.WbflvYqQyuU

2 Ibid.

3 Rachel Sklar, "David Remnick on that New Yorker Cover: It's Satire, Meant to Target 'Distortions and Misconceptions and Prejudices' about Obama", *Huffington Post*, 21 July 2006.

4 Françoise Mouly, *Blown Covers: New Yorker Covers You Were Never Meant to See*, Abrams, 2012, p.57.

5 Interview with Ian Birch.

6 The satirical news show on Comedy Central hosted by Jon Stewart ran a collage of clips from Fox, ABC, CBS, NBC and CNN that clearly suggested Obama could be a Muslim.

PRICE $4.50

JULY 21, 2008

THE NEW YORKER

2010s

TIME

9 AUGUST 2010

Managing editor: Rick Stengel

Pakistan/Afghanistan correspondent:
 Aryn Baker

Director of photography & visual enterprise:
 Kira Pollack

Cover photography: Jodi Bieber

"The Taliban pounded on the door just before midnight, demanding that Aisha, 18, be punished for running away from her husband's house. They dragged her to a mountain clearing near her village in the southern Afghan province of Uruzgan, ignoring her protests that her in-laws had been abusive, that she had no choice but to escape ... Her judge, a local Taliban commander, was unmoved ... The commander gave his verdict, and men moved in to deliver the punishment. Aisha's brother-in-law held her down while her husband pulled out a knife. First he sliced off her ears. Then he started on her nose. Aisha passed out from the pain but awoke soon after, choking on her own blood. The men had left her on the mountainside to die," wrote Aryn Baker in the opening paragraphs of her cover story.[1]

JODI BIEBER:

Aisha was in the "Women for Afghan Women" shelter. I had to photograph her there. Shay, my wonderful translator, and I arrived at ten in the morning. We went into a small room where a lot of young women slept. There was a red carpet with scattered cushions around the wall, a radio and one white fan. There was nothing to say, "This is Aisha's space."

I started photographing her but I didn't feel it coming together. I put my camera down and said to her, "Try to think of your inner beauty and your inner strength. I know you'll never forget what happened to you but I want you to try feel your power." She looked up, looked at me in that way, and I took the photo.

Inside: Joe Klein on the challenge in Pakistan

TIME

What Happens if We Leave Afghanistan

BY ARYN BAKER

Aisha, 18, had her nose and ears cut off last year on orders from the Taliban because she fled abusive in-laws

I thought I had failed because I didn't show her ears in the photograph. I didn't show her as vulnerable. I thought, *Time* isn't going to like the photograph. I was very worried.

KIRA POLLACK:

The picture came in, and I was blown away. I thought, "Wow, what would happen if it became the cover? I showed it to a few top editors, including Nancy Gibbs who was deputy editor at the time. Her feeling was: "What does this do to a child who sees it for the first time? This might be the most violent image a child has ever seen."

Each editor had a different point of view. A lot of people thought it was too much for the cover. Then we showed it to Rick. He was very thoughtful and silent. He did not say no. He brought it home for the weekend. He wanted to see what his wife and two sons, who were then nine and twelve, thought of it. On Monday he said, "I want to do this on the cover."

JODI BIEBER:

It didn't stop there. The headline, "What Happens if We Leave Afghanistan", caused a complete controversy.[2] I was on every TV station you could imagine. Even the Taliban wrote something denying that they were involved. An academic – I think she was from Cambridge – said, how could I objectify Aisha, that she had had her hair done and that I photographed her in a studio. It was so not the truth. People in the West said it was war pornography. And then it won the World Press Photo of the Year 2010.

But Aisha did get to America for a series of reconstructive surgeries at the Walter Reed Hospital in Washington. When you look at the photograph, I think you first see her beauty and then you see her nose. For me, it's about beauty and the beast, the darkness and the light. It's not a record of her; it's an interpretation of her and that could only have come from me. Aisha now lives with an Afghan-American family in the U.S.

---

1 Condensed from Aryn Baker, "What Happens If We Leave Afghanistan", *Time*, 9 August 2010.
2 The lack of a question mark added fuel to the fire of the controversy. As Rod Norland wrote in *The New York Times* on 4 August 2010: "Reaction to the *Time* cover has become something of an Internet litmus test about attitudes toward the war, and what America's responsibility is in Afghanistan. Critics of the American presence in Afghanistan call it 'emotional blackmail' and even 'war porn', while those who fear the consequences of abandoning Afghanistan see it as a powerful appeal to conscience."

VICE

MARCH 2012

Editor-in-chief: Rocco Castoro

Managing editor: Ellis Jones

Art director: Matt Schoen

Photo editor: Serena Pezzato

Cover photography: Maurizio Cattelan
    & Pierpaolo Ferrari

Launched in Montreal in 1994, the now-global free monthly *Vice* was a wildly renegade source of news for millennials. Cover images were extreme, defiant, outlandish. This trio of a toilet plunger, stapler and dildo was created by the Italian artist Maurizio Cattelan and photographer Pierpaolo Ferrari, who together had recently launched *Toiletpaper,* a surrealist bi-annual. For American distribution, *Vice* had to cover the dildo with a peel-off sticker. The UK published it untamed (Figure 14), while Australia, France, Spain and the Netherlands went with an alternative image of cigarette stubs in pink ice cream, also by Cattelan and Ferrari.

ELLIS JONES:

We called this one "The Holy Trinity" issue. Our photo editor then, Serena, helped bring it in for us.

SERENA PEZZATO:

I was a big fan of *Toiletpaper,* so I asked them if they would be interested in having some images published in *Vice.* They said they'd be happy to give us an exclusive preview of the forthcoming issue plus some outtakes. Everyone at *Vice* was super-excited. Maurizio felt very strongly about going with the dildo image because he and Pierpaolo knew that only *Vice* could pull it off. Not many other "regular" magazines could put something like that on the cover and not lose some of their advertisers and/or get criticized by readers and other media. It made sense to everyone at *Vice,* so we saw this as an opportunity to provoke – and to amuse – and to do it together with two incredible artists.

FREE
VOLUME 19 NUMBER 3

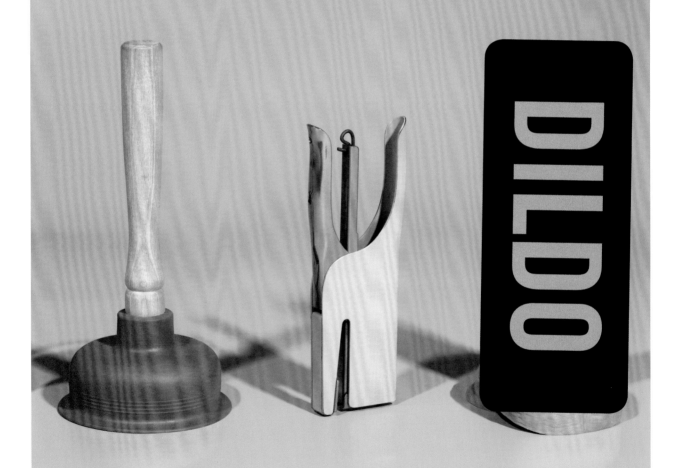

DILDO

VICE

FREE
VOLUME 10 NUMBER 3

The only concerns were about the shipping company potentially blocking the magazine deliveries to the subscribers because of the dildo, so we decided to cover it with a sticker. Matt designed the classic censor bar and it worked perfectly. I suggested to write the word "DILDO" on it to play a joke on the whole idea of censorship – rendering the bar a bit useless by saying what was underneath. Maurizio loved it.

I think we all felt like rascals carving a "dirty" drawing on the school desk. Personally, I liked the image because of its simplicity: in a way, it "equalizes" the three objects, so you are invited to forget about their functions and see them for what they are: inanimate material elements in different shapes. On the other hand, the dildo is placed there precisely to disrupt this abstraction and put your brain in a short circuit – a funny one.

MATT SCHOEN:

The sticker was one of those problem-solves that felt less like a compromise and actually helped the issue. When the magazine was distributed in New York, for about a month you would see dildo stickers on signs all over the city.

Figure 14 The cover without its censor bar sticker included.

TIME

21 MAY 2012

Managing editor: Rick Stengel
Design director: D W Pine III
Director of photography and visual
    enterprise: Kira Pollack
Cover photography: Martin Schoeller

This *Time* cover, for a story on attachment parenting, featured 26-year-old Jamie Lynne Grumet of Los Angeles and her son Aram, aged 3. It sparked a firestorm of comments, many of them negative: it was seen as offensive, exploitative, psychologically abusive, a shocking ploy to sell copies and a shameless attempt to stoke up the "mommy wars". Grumet's blog crashed with the weight of traffic. Seth Meyers on *Saturday Night Live* pointed out to *Time* that if they "wanted a great cover, you would have Photoshopped out the chair", which he did and showed the child hanging in mid-air. Seventy-three per cent of respondents to a Today.com poll said they didn't want to see the photograph in the first place.[1]

Managing editor Rick Stengel took to the media to defend the magazine. He told the *Washington Post*: "It's certainly an arresting image. It's an image to get people's attention about a serious subject. Judging by the reaction on Twitter this morning, some people think it's great, and some people are revolted by it."[2]

KIRA POLLACK:
It was a very hard shoot. There were so many awkward parts to the picture. It was a Sunday and the issue was going to close in two days.

MARTIN SCHOELLER:
I wasn't sure how to feel at first about photographing a woman breastfeeding, but it became more intriguing when I heard the child would be an almost

The French Rejection 26

God of Cricket 40

TIME

ARE YOU
MOM
ENOUGH?

Why attachment
parenting drives some
mothers to extremes—
and how Dr. Bill Sears
became their guru

BY KATE PICKERT

**Jamie Lynne
Grumet, 26, and
her 3-year-old son**

four-year-old boy. Especially considering my own son of the same age had not been breastfed for maybe three years by that point.

First I thought I'd do a Madonna breastfeeding kind of portrait, something with a spiritual feeling, but when I pictured how big this boy would look sitting on his mom's lap, I thought him standing would be the most amazing position to emphasize his age. I brought in my son's chair and he stood on that. The boy's dad was a Special Forces police officer, hence the camouflage pants. He was a full-grown kid, running around playing hunting bad guys with his dad in the backyard.

KIRA POLLACK:
Jamie's husband was very big, and she was very petite, and her son took after her husband. So, while he looks a lot older than he is, and he did the day he was born, that juxtaposition really worked well.

MARTIN SCHOELLER:
When I took the picture, it seemed so natural that he was breastfeeding. The mother and son were both happy to do it. Later it dawned on me how controversial this could be. Some people get more upset about breastfeeding than about gun violence. I was surprised by how vilely some people reacted. We all constantly see crazy, gratuitous violence in film and television, but somehow breastfeeding is off limits. That's terrible.

---

1   Quoted on https://thesocietypages.org/
    socimages/2012/05/30/controversy-over-times-are-
    you-mom-enough-cover/
2   Quoted in Brian Braiker, "*Time* breastfeeding cover
    ignites debate around 'attachment parenting'", the
    Guardian US news blog, 10 May 2012. https://www.
    theguardian.com/world/us-news-blog/2012/may/10/
    time-magazine-breastfeeding

THE GENTLEWOMAN

AUTUMN AND WINTER 2012

Editor-in-chief: Penny Martin
Art direction and design: Veronica Ditting
Cover photography: Terry Richardson

In 2010 independent Dutch publishers Gert Jonkers and Jop van Bennekom followed their influential bi-annual men's fashion magazine, *Fantastic Man*, with a bi-annual for women, recruiting Penny Martin to help them. This watershed cover paired two very different artists: the 46-year-old provocative fashion photographer Terry Richardson and 86-year-old acting royalty Angela Lansbury. Martin remembers the session as affectionate, funny and mutually respectful.

PENNY MARTIN:

We felt we had to be an antidote to what was out in the market at the time. There was a kind of pornography of femininity in women's magazines. You felt overly familiar with the look of women but you also felt that they were silenced. There was a sense of mediation by the agent, by the retoucher, by the photographer.

We wanted the cover to be a compliment to the sitter. Their personality was first and foremost. We didn't want them to be treated like a makeover where they feel like they're going to be made a fool of, put into clothes they'd never wear, and have their hair and make-up done so they don't look recognizable, and feel like a drag act. Angela was photographed at home in New York in her own clothing.

We needed warm, candid, funny. I'd seen a lot of photographs that Terry Richardson had taken of his mother,[1] and they were respectful and fun. I just felt that he would treat her like somebody who has a lot to say. Angela put on Terry's glasses. That happened on the spur of the moment, though it's a leitmotif that runs through many of his portraits and a kind of hallmark of Angela being

the gentlewoman

Fabulous women's magazine, issue n° 6
Autumn and Winter 2012

9 771879 869012

03

UK £6.00

USA $14.99

Angela Lansbury

in on the fun, not feeling like she's projected onto. Her glance says, "I know that you know that I know." It's a really complicit exchange. And she knows she looks fabulous. It's like, "I look hot, and you know it."

When an older woman is photographed in a woman's consumer title, it is often from the side, a bit like a Pietà. Suddenly, it's the really serious piece in the editorial well and it takes all the heat out of the shot. The girls get to be hot and carefree, and the older woman becomes the *grande dame*.

When the pictures came in, there was a kind of strange moment. I don't think it's happened before where we looked at them and started howling with laughter. People love that picture. It's a celebration of female role models, women of purpose. It's almost a political statement.

That cover changed everything. It summed up every ambition we had for *The Gentlewoman* in one shot. It sold like crazy and is one of our most reproduced images. I expected our commercial supporters to feel slightly quizzical about it. The big surprise was when I walked into showrooms in Italy, they'd go, *"Ah, la signora in giallo!"* – the Italian name for *Murder, She Wrote*.[2]

1 See *Mom/Dad*, Morel Books, 2010.
2 American crime drama TV series (1984–96) starring Angela Lansbury.

NEW YORK

12 NOVEMBER 2012

Editor: Adam Moss
Design director: Thomas Alberty
Photography director: Jody Quon
Cover photograph: "New York City,
    October 31" by Iwan Baan

Hurricane Sandy hit the New York region on Monday 29 October, causing a massive power outage. Tellingly, the Goldman Sachs Tower, and the immediate area around it in Lower Manhattan, continued to burn brightly. After 9/11, the finance company had invested in extensive protection against another possible catastrophe. For many, however, there was "nothing so richly symbolic as this display of literal power".[1]

ADAM MOSS:

It was during the last presidential election[2] where the haves and have-nots were a huge theme, and it occurred to us that the theme was also playing out, in a different way, in New York City, where half the city was enshrouded in darkness and half in the light. Jody, who's quite a genius, felt that there was an opportunity to actually capture that by helicopter.

JODY QUON:

On Wednesday morning I said, "We need to take the picture tonight." I didn't know when the power was going to go back on. I knew Iwan took pictures from the air. He's based in Amsterdam, but really he's like a vagabond. He happened to be in town to take pictures of the Parrish Art Museum in Eastern Long Island from the air for its architects, Herzog & de Meuron. He couldn't do it because the museum grounds were flooded. He said he'd love to do this. I said to him, "It'd be great to shoot it from the southernmost tip so that you can get a sense of the blackness, and then you get the lights."

I had not gone through a situation like this before. There were so many variables that I hadn't even thought about, but Iwan had. One was cash machines, which were no longer functioning. He had taken out a few thousand dollars, so he had the cash to charter a helicopter from a company out in Eastern Long Island that was still functioning.

Two, he had already reserved a rental car at the airport so he had wheels to get him out to Long Island. The trains were not functioning.

Is that unbelievable? It gets better. Normally, helicopters can only fly at a certain altitude because of all the planes from La Guardia, Newark and Kennedy. It's very dangerous. But the airports were closed so the pilot got special permission to go higher, so Iwan could get the right angle for the picture. Also, Canon had, by chance, loaned him the most sophisticated, state-of-the-art digital camera.

NEW YORK

The City and the Storm

Starting on p.17

$5.99 USA/CANADA

NYMAG.COM

0 71658 01912 6

4 7

I remember looking at them with Adam the next morning. I was emotional, "Oh, my God, he made the picture."

IWAN BAAN:
The chances for this picture coming together were like one per cent.

When the power went out, I had this impulse to photograph the division in the city: those with power and light, next to those left powerless and in the dark. I've flown above New York countless times, so while on the ground, I knew exactly what I wanted to capture.

A heli-pilot who wasn't on a rescue mission agreed to take me up – if I could make my way to Long Island. While I was driving out there, Jody called me. In the short moment I had her on the phone before the line got disconnected I understood she had the same idea.

I had just acquired the Canon 1D X, which was at that time the most sensitive camera available. Until the 1D X, most cameras had an ISO of 1600 or 3200, but this one could go up to 51200 – meaning I could photograph in almost complete darkness from a vibrating and shaky helicopter.

My work revolves around the built environment: from the commissions I get from architects to the work I do on cities and how they grow, and how people adapt to many different environments. I try to remind people how fragile things can be, and how they can change in a moment. This was one of those unique moments we were able to capture.

ADAM MOSS:
It doesn't look like a magazine cover. It just looks like an amazing picture. When we faded out the logo and did the tiny little headline, it suddenly became a cover and told the story vividly. The response was huge. MoMA made a poster of it.[3]

1 Jessica Pressler, "Goldman Has the Power", *New York*, 12 November 2012, p.26.
2 The 2012 election between Democrat Barack Obama and Republican Mitt Romney.
3 All proceeds from the poster were donated to the Mayor's Fund to Advance New York City to support Hurricane Sandy relief efforts.

BLOOMBERG BUSINESSWEEK

15–21 JULY 2013
Editor-in-chief: Josh Tyrangiel
Creative director: Richard Turley
Deputy photo editor: Emily Keegan
Features art director: Jaci Kessler

Hedge funders weren't happy with this conflation of high finance and low masculinity on the front cover of *Bloomberg Businessweek*. Josh Tyrangiel issued a statement: "The cover highlights the macho mythology of hedge fund managers, whose returns over the past decade have lagged behind the S&P 500. Yes, we're making them the butt of a joke; we're pretty sure they can take it."[1] There was another cover option – a story on Sears – but, as Turley later said, "It seemed very difficult to escape from this idea once it was hatched."[2]

In 2014 the magazine won a coveted Yellow Pencil at the D&AD (Design and Art Direction) Awards for a series of five covers in 2013 that included this one.

RICHARD TURLEY:

This wasn't just my cover. I did a drawing of a guy with a big penis based on an old *Rolling Stone* campaign, "Perception versus Reality".[3] Huge penis the perception; small penis the reality. Jaci and Emily then got involved.

JACI KESSLER:

I thought about a man standing in front of a chart that happened to have fever lines sprouting from the crotch area. It was clearly representative of penises but using totally mundane graphics.

I couldn't find the perfect guy, and we didn't have time to shoot a character model, so he's made of two stock images: one for his head and one for his body. I didn't want him to look macho or sexual at all, and he had to be fully clothed,

July 15 — July 21, 2013 | businessweek.com

Bloomberg Businessweek

Perception

The Hedge Fund Myth p8

Reality

slightly perplexed, unassuming. Although most people probably wouldn't think spending hours searching Getty Images for "man + middle-aged + collared shirt + profile view" is much fun, I loved it.

The arrows started off looking pretty standard – I was trying to have their placement tell the whole story. Richard kept pushing me to make the green one thicker and more rounded. Once that was decided, the red one got droopier and more pathetic-looking until we ended up with this. But I did want it to look pieced together, which is why I went with a flat, bold graphic for the arrows and a black-and-white halftone photo.

RICHARD TURLEY:

Everyone who saw it laughed, which is always a good thing. Josh wrote the cover lines. He had to have a couple of discussions with management but, in the end, they liked it too. There were only 2,000 hedge funders so we didn't care about their reaction.

JACI KESSLER:

I liked that a lot of people thought that we legitimately did not realize what we had done, which is ridiculous.

1   Seth Fiegerman, "'*Businessweek*' Cover May Excite Readers a Little Too Much", *Mashable*, 11 July 2013. http://mashable.com/2013/07/11/businessweek-hedge-fund-cover/#Oud6Yj4p4Gqu
2   "Bloomberg Creative Director Richard Turley dishes on 'The Hedge Fund Myth'" by Katie Myrick Parks, *Society for News Design*, 16 July 2013
3   Landmark advertising campaign created by Fallon in 1985.

ROLLING STONE

1 AUGUST 2013

Editor and publisher: Jann S Wenner
Managing editor: Will Dana
Design director: Joseph Hutchinson
Creative director: Jodi Peckman
Cover photo illustration: Sean McCabe
Cover story: Janet Reitman

On 15 April 2013, two homemade pressure cooker bombs exploded near the Boston Marathon's finishing line in Boylston Street. It was a scene of carnage: three people were killed and more than 250 injured. Police identified brothers Tamerlan and Dzhokhar Tsarnaev as suspects. Four days later, after a shootout which resulted in Tamerlan's death, 19-year-old Dzhokhar was captured, and formally charged on 22 April. *Rolling Stone* investigated. The magazine had a long and award-winning history of in-depth hard news stories. It published the cover online before the article which put the immediate focus on Dzhokar's picture – the same picture that *The New York Times*, for example, had run on its front page of 5 May 2013 with no backlash.

Rolling Stone faced a barrage of abuse and criticism: that it glamorized a suspected terrorist; that by cropping in on his tousled hair, brooding eyes and Armani Exchange T-shirt, it turned him into a kind of young Jim Morrison; that it endorsed Tsarnaev in the sense that a *Rolling Stone* cover denotes success and confers cultural importance. Some asked why the victims weren't on the cover. Others pointed out that Tsarnaev hadn't been convicted yet and that "The Bomber" cover line seemed to forget that a person is innocent until proven guilty. Boston Mayor Tom Menino suspected *Rolling Stone* had done it for publicity. CVS, the pharmacy chain, would not sell the issue "out of respect for the victims of the attack and their loved ones".

Rolling Stone issued a statement: "Our hearts go out to the victims of the Boston Marathon bombing, and our thoughts are always with them and their families. The cover story we are publishing this week falls within the traditions of journalism and *Rolling Stone*'s long-standing commitment to serious and thoughtful coverage of the most important political and cultural issues of our day. The fact that Dzhokhar Tsarnaev is young, and in the same age group as many of our readers, makes it all the more important for us to examine the complexities of this issue and gain a more complete understanding of how a tragedy like this happens." The issue doubled its newsstand sale.

JANN WENNER:

That was the news picture. It was an old photograph of that kid. I mean he looked so young and cute and innocent and that was the point of the story – the innocence of youth. It got us in an enormous amount of trouble because he looked so innocent.

I guess because he had long hair people say he looked like a pop star. If it had been on some other magazine other than *Rolling Stone* they wouldn't have said that. He's a kid who got caught in this turmoil, the system and lack of opportunity, and his brother's madness, and got torn apart.

JODI PECKMAN:

The image is from his Facebook page and was by no means something the entire world hadn't seen already. The decision to use it on the cover was simple. It was the only one that would have worked for clarity and instant recognizability. Not much else existed.

It wasn't meant to be the cover of that particular issue, but the story was huge. We had exclusive material and Janet Reitman, one of our best reporters, wrote it. So we went with this cover.

Sean didn't do much to the image, just enhanced it for clarity. It was a muddy image and he may have put a slight filter on it. We were blowing it up so big that some sharpening – for lack of a better word – was needed. There was no discussion about making him look better. It was more about trying to make it print better.

I had a hard time understanding the response. I mean, I understood the way people felt about this guy, but we didn't put him on the cover to make him look like a rock star. We put him on the cover because he was news, the same way we put Charles Manson on the cover back in the Seventies.[1] It's not like we liked the guy, for Chrissake.

1 *Rolling Stone* 61, 25 June 1970.

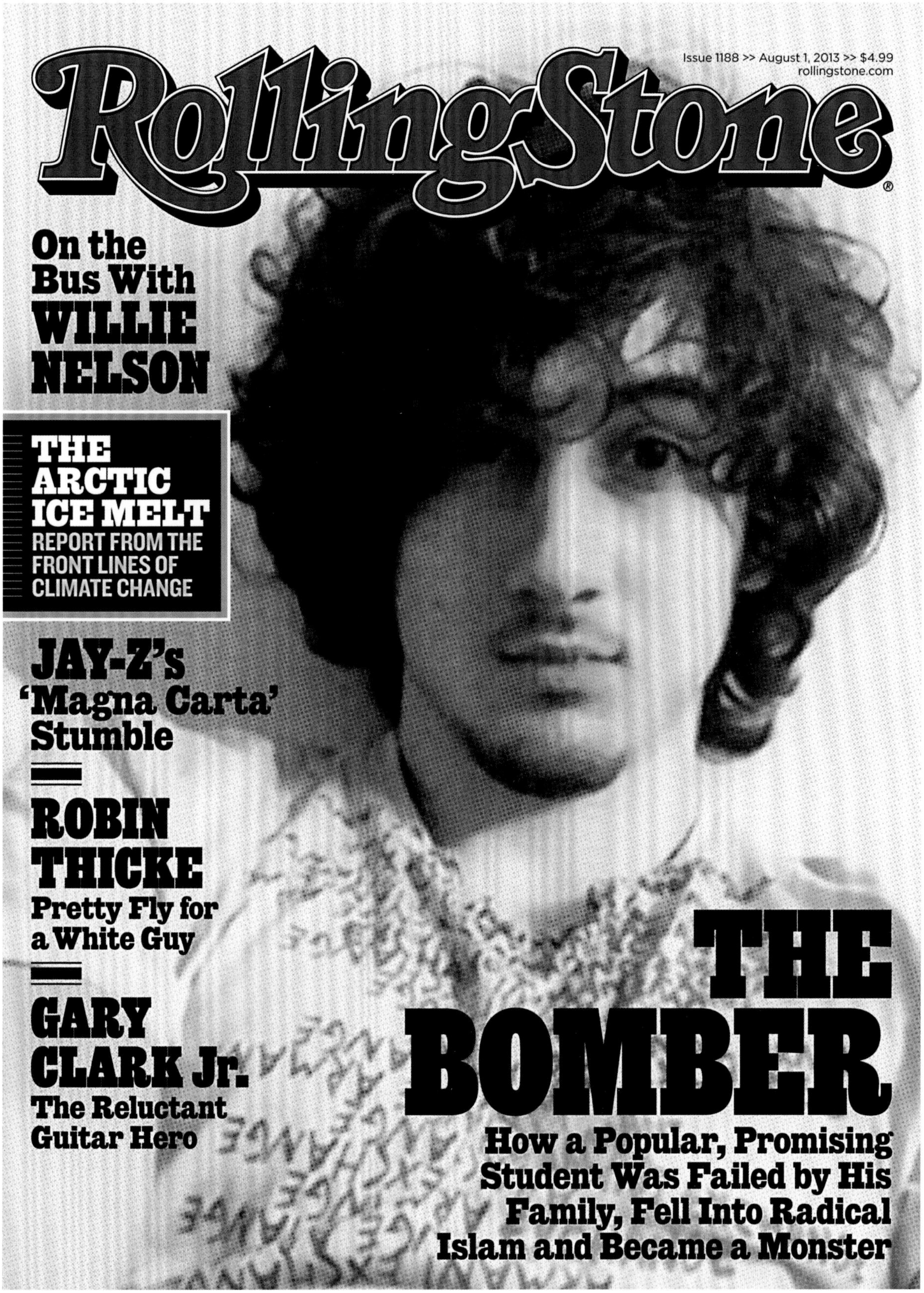

RollingStone

Issue 1188 >> August 1, 2013 >> $4.99
rollingstone.com

On the
Bus With
**WILLIE
NELSON**

THE ARCTIC ICE MELT
REPORT FROM THE
FRONT LINES OF
CLIMATE CHANGE

**JAY-Z's
'Magna Carta'
Stumble**

**ROBIN
THICKE**
Pretty Fly for
a White Guy

**GARY
CLARK Jr.**
The Reluctant
Guitar Hero

THE BOMBER

**How a Popular, Promising
Student Was Failed by His
Family, Fell Into Radical
Islam and Became a Monster**

O

THE OPR
MAGAZI

AN O EXTRAVAGANZA!

Let's Talk About
HAIR!

Everything You Need to Know to

- Grow It • Blow It • Awesomely 'Fro It
- Boost the Bounce • Beat the Frizz
- Handle the Gray and...

Have a Great Hair Day!

The Guilt-Free Snack, pg. 114

What's *Really* Healthy Surprising News From Dr. Oz

Spread Too Thin? Smart Advice for the Seriously Frazzled

She Smokes, She Smooches, She Dances in Bell-Bottoms! Behind the Scenes of Oprah's New Movie

O, THE OPRAH MAGAZINE

SEPTEMBER 2013

Founder and editorial director:
   Oprah Winfrey
Editor-in-chief: Lucy Kaylin
Creative director: Adam Glassman
Cover photography: Ruven Afanador

A full afro had not been seen on the cover of a mainstream American women's magazine in a while. *O* was launched in April 2000 by Hearst and Oprah Winfrey, the entertainment mogul and philanthropist. This image of the magazine's founder hit a national nerve, prompted "Froprah" mania and clocked up over 337 million media impressions.[1] The issue won two National Magazine Awards in 2014.[2]

LUCY KAYLIN:

The topic of hair is often handled in a superficial way, despite its deeply personal, psychological and political implications. And every ethnicity has its own hair issues – something we wanted to explore for our very diverse readership. The idea was to start a big, fun, frank conversation about something that's on all of our minds.

As for the cover, we thought, "Let's see if Oprah would collaborate on a really bold hair moment". Adam Glassman, our cover magician, knew a wig maker, Kim Kimble, who'd no doubt come up with something cool. Andre Walker, Oprah's long-time hairstylist, was the "wig wrangler", and did an amazing job making it look natural on Oprah. Luckily, our cover model was very much into it. That was the secret sauce: Oprah's enthusiasm.

ADAM GLASSMAN:

We made it as big and curly as possible. It was like, "OK, I want to be liberated and wear my hair natural like it is when I come out of the shower." We'll do an exaggerated version of that. That conversation about wearing your hair more naturally really started after this cover.

The wig came in bubble wrap on a headstand in a special bright-pink travel box. It was like the unveiling of the crown jewels. We listened over and over again to the soundtrack of *The Lion King*. Oprah wanted that because she felt like this lioness with this mane of hair. I originally wanted it really stripped down, no jewellery at all, but Oprah is a jewellery person.

When we showed it to people before we went to press, they were very divided by it. Some asked if it was too much of a political statement. It really was not the intention.

LUCY KAYLIN:

That day on the set was just a blast. Oprah looked gorgeous when this 3lb wig landed on her head. She called it "wild thing". The wig was almost like another person. It required care and feeding.

This cover had the drama, the joy, the edge, the beauty that I wished for, and readers loved it. A lot of women of colour thought it was very liberating for this particular hairstyle to be celebrated in this manner because, of course, we all remember a time when to have a fully grown-out afro was a political decision. Along with a lot of other things from the 1960s and 1970s it was associated with racial strife. In the ensuing years, a lot of women of colour decided on their own or, in some cases, felt pressure to straighten their hair or subdue their curls, and that has a socio-political edge to it. This cover was "Yeah, this is beautiful."

Chris Rock really was an impetus for us. As he so smartly laid out in his documentary,[3] our hair is a deep and divisive and difficult issue. That's why this cover came across as this clarion call. It was celebrating the fact it's all good: you be you, have fun with whatever's growing out of your head.

1 Sourced from "Best Cover Contest 2014 Winners & Finalists", *ASME (American Society of Magazine Editors)* website. http://www.magazine.org/asme/magazine-cover-contest/past-winners-finalists/2014-winners-finalists

2 For "Leisure Interests" and "Best Cover Contest" in the Women's Service section.

3 *Good Hair* (dir. Jeff Stilson, 2009), narrated by Chris Rock.

THE BIG ISSUE

**"REMEMBRANCE DAY" SPECIAL,
3 NOVEMBER 2014**

Editor: Paul McNamee
Cover photograph: Bryan Adams
Cover subject: Sgt Rick Clement

Remembrance Day, which honours those in the armed forces who died in the line of duty, has a special resonance for *The Big Issue*. Between 8 and 10 per cent of its street vendors are ex-forces. The year 2014 was even more poignant, when the commemoration observed three major conflicts – the 100th anniversary of the start of World War I, the 70th anniversary of the D-Day landings, and the end of Britain's conflict in Afghanistan.

PAUL MCNAMEE:

I wanted something about the here and now, about men and women who had come back from serving with life-altering injuries. Not those who died serving, but those who have to live with incredible problems.

Through some weird links, I got to know Bryan Adams who had a book called *Wounded*.[1] He had spent time photographing the injuries of soldiers who had lost limbs – or much worse. I asked him if we could we use some of his imagery. He agreed and I settled on that particular image of Sgt Rick Clement, who lost his legs in Afghanistan in 2010 when he stepped on a Taliban roadside explosive device. He lost everything below the waist and died twice as docs fought to save him. His injuries were so severe that he shouldn't have been alive.

It's such a brilliant, arresting photograph. When you look at it first, you see a man in a dress uniform, sitting down. Then you realize he has no legs: his body is cut in half. I thought, that's the reality of what we're talking about. They go away as happy young boys and they come back with no limbs. It's classic-looking but at the same time shocking.

It was shortlisted for the PPA[2] Awards "British Cover of the Year", which is voted for by the public. We won. I think people reacted very honestly to it. They weren't looking at it professionally, saying things like "That's the right point size." So that was particularly good.

There was an incredibly emotional outpouring from everybody, a standing ovation, as Rick accepted the award with Bryan. Rick was delighted. He's quite deadpan. He said, "It's great to be in a room where there's more people legless than I am." I imagine that's a line he's used before but it's still a good line.

When he was in the rehabilitation hospital, he said he was determined to walk, and they said, "There's no chance, nothing exists for this." But they developed very expensive advanced prosthetics legs for him so he could actually stand up. He wanted to walk to the Cenotaph for the following Remembrance Sunday – and he did. That meant that the next year we could do a cover of him standing up. So the circle of the story was completed.

1   Bryan Adams, *Wounded: The Legacy of War. Photographs by Bryan Adams*, Steidl 2013.
2   Professional Publishers Association.

**This is now.
We must not forget.**

THE BIG ISSUE

EVERY MONDAY £2.50

SERGEANT RICK CLEMENT, 34

LONDON | November 3-9, 2014 No.1127 | A HAND UP NOT A HANDOUT

ESSENCE

FEBRUARY 2015

Editor-in-chief: Vanessa K. De Luca
Creative director: Erika N Perry

#BLACKLIVESMATTER surfaced in 2013. The brainchild of Alicia Garza, Patrisse Cullors and Opal Tometi, it quickly became a rallying call for the black community to protest against racial inequality and police brutality. When 12-year-old Tamir Rice died from a gunshot wound in Cleveland in November 2014, *Essence*, the respected monthly for African American women, decided that it had to take a stand. They "invited activists, thought leaders and cultural figures to reflect on the meaning of this moment, and what we must do next".[1] It was their first celebrity-free, pure-type cover since their launch in 1970.

VANESSA K. DE LUCA:

One of our junior editors reached out to me and said, "How are we going to address this? We are all reeling from what it's doing to our community, what it's doing to our own psyches." I called the editors together and we started challenging each other about what we could do, what we should do. Could this be a cover? Can we do this under this corporate umbrella of Time Inc., quite honestly?

We couldn't agree, but that was a good thing because it meant that we're not all monolithic in how we see this BLACKLIVESMATTER idea. There were people who felt we should go all the way, radical. There were others who felt like no, there are ways to utilize this moment to drive change within existing social structures, within the justice system. It's like comparing the Black Panthers and Martin Luther King Jr. It's like two totally different parts of the spectrum.

We thought we have to try to find voices that represent all of those things. And it's up to the audience to decide where you land. It really was as if somebody pumped new life and breath into each one of us. We made our dream list of people. We had young people from the New York Justice League. We had the three young women who invented the hashtag. We had Reverend Al Sharpton for a different perspective as a civil rights leader and icon. We had Pulitzer Prize-winning author Isabel Wilkerson, who wrote a beautiful opening essay. We had Common and John Legend, who were extremely topical because of the movie *Selma*[2] and their song "Glory" that was up for an Oscar. It worked out well for us that February was Black History Month.

Erika and I finally decided on a pure-type cover. I thought, "As this is the first time we're doing this, let's go for broke," and it very easily became black and white with the hint of red. The treatment is graphic and spare in an issue that is just fraught with so much emotion. We wanted it to be in your face. Like you cannot turn away. This was not about selling anyone anything. It was about we want to do something – could this be a start?

We had over 41 million media impressions with people sharing the cover on Instagram, and black Twitter going crazy. Shonda Rhimes shot me an email and just said, "Yes." This is where our vision and our values came together quite clearly.

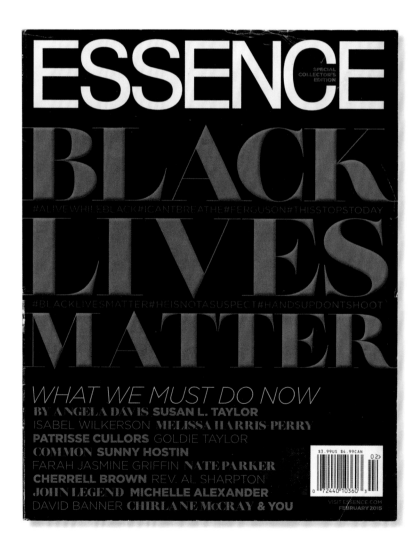

1 Introduction to the cover feature, "Black Lives Matter", February 2015, p.90.
2 *Selma* (dir. Ava DuVerney) was based on the voting rights marches from Selma to Montgomery in 1965. It was released in the USA on 9 January 2015.

ZEIT MAGAZIN

28 MAY 2015

Editor-in-chief: Christoph Amend

Creative director: Mirko Borsche

Art director: Jasmin Müller-Stoy

Designer: Mirko Merkel

Guest editor: Mohamed Amjahid

Cover caption: "Every day, people start out in the hope of a better life. We dedicate this issue to you. An especially large number of the refugees coming to Germany are from Arab countries /That's why ZEIT magazine appears in German and Arabic."

Weekly newspaper *Die Zeit* launched Germany's first magazine supplement in 1970. Christoph Amend, who became editor in May 2007, introduced a double cover, two consecutive photographs, illustrations or type treatments that make a pithy point. This was a special on refugees that Simon Kuper from the *Financial Times Weekend* read "open-mouthed" because it "presented refugees not as helpless mute victims on sinking boats but as grown-up humans with insights into their adopted country".[1]

CHRISTOPH AMEND:

I had the idea in the last days of 2014 when I read the first reports about refugees making their way to Central Europe. To edit, design and produce the issue was highly sensitive, so we hired Mohamed as a guest editor.

MOHAMED AMJAHID:

All the text had something to do with the new lives of refugees in Germany: learning a new language, fighting German bureaucracy, getting over homesickness and facing racism. The issue featured many new citizens, not only those from Arabic-speaking countries. However, *Zeit Magazin* decided to publish the texts in Arabic and German since most of the arriving people in 2015 spoke Arabic as their mother language.

JASMIN MÜLLER-STOY:

We split every page into two. Arabic type is read from right to left so it was difficult to lay out because our InDesign wasn't able to type the Arabic font in the right direction. We had to figure out how to turn the cover in one direction so you can read it as German, and turn it in the other direction to read it as Arabic.

MOHAMED AMJAHID:

I sometimes turned the monitors upside down because it was easier or I printed the pages out, putting them in the middle of the room and running in circles.

I am one of the few German journalists who speak Arabic as a mother language and I was the only one at the magazine who could read the issue. I felt a huge pressure. It was hard to translate the texts so they correspond and make sense at the same time.

JASMIN MÜLLER-STOY:

It was tricky to choose a colour for the cover. We first thought about green, but not all Arabian countries have green in their flag and we didn´t want anybody to feel excluded. So we decided to take a neutral colour. Yellow seemed to be perfect. Mohammed helped us find a font which looked modern.

We had this idea to use the first pictures that refugees took in Germany inside. The refugees really appreciated this gesture. We tried to do extra copies so they could get them. We took the magazine to several refugee camps in Germany.

MOHAMED AMJAHID:

Was there a message? Refugees welcome. Many German subscribers were amazed. Of course, some right-wing supporters complained that "their Germany will disappear now" because we had published in Arabic.

CHRISTOPH AMEND:

We never had so many requests from organizations and schools for extra copies. Friends from the magazine industry in New York wrote, saying, "We could never do that in America." It was quite a ride to publish half of a magazine that you can't read yourself.

---

1 *Financial Times Weekend*, 19 June 2015.

Jeden Tag machen sich Menschen auf den Weg, in der Hoffnung auf ein besseres Leben. Ihnen widmen wir dieses Heft. Besonders viele Flüchtlinge kommen aus arabischen Ländern nach Deutschland

ZEIT ❧ MAGAZIN

ZEIT ⚜ MAGAZIN

Nʀ. 22, 28. Mᴀɪ 2015

Deshalb erscheint dieses ZEITmagazin
auf Deutsch und Arabisch

ﺟﻤﺎﻻﺕ ﻋﺪﺩ ﻫﺬﺍ ﺍﻟﻌﺪﺩ ﻣﻦ ZEITmagazin
ﺑﺎﻟﻠﻐﺘﻴﻦ ﺍﻷﻟﻤﺎﻧﻴﺔ ﻭ ﺍﻟﻌﺮﺑﻴﺔ

2015 ﻣﺎﻳﻮ/ﺃﻳﺎﺭ 28 ، 22 ﻋﺪﺩ

ZEIT ⚜ MAGAZIN

VANITY FAIR

"Call me Caitlyn"

By BUZZ BISSINGER *Photos by* ANNIE LEIBOVITZ

VANITY FAIR

JULY 2015

Editor: Graydon Carter
Features editor: Jane Sarkin
Fashion and style director: Jessica Diehl
Deputy editor: Dana Brown
Associate managing director: Ellen Kiell
Photograph of Caitlyn Jenner by
    Annie Leibovitz, styled by Jessica Diehl.

This was a milestone: the first cover with an openly transgender woman – Caitlyn Jenner. For the previous 65 years she had lived as Bruce Jenner, all-American hero, Olympic gold medallist and, most recently, reality TV star. To safeguard its exclusive, the magazine implemented a military-style level of planning and security. Only eight people knew about it and they could only use one computer, which was always offline, to work on the gigantic 11,000-word, 22-page feature. Condé Nast claims that more than 46 million people accessed content that related to the cover story on social media within the first 24 hours. The issue sold more than 430,000 on the newsstand, making it *Vanity Fair*'s best-selling issue for five years.

CAITLYN JENNER:

It was a very long decision with a lot of people, family, friends, relatives, God, my pastor. So many people who deal with gender dysphoria can sneak away, do what they have to do to live their life authentically, and then slowly work their way back into life, but because I was getting destroyed by the tabloids, I couldn't do that. It was so important that it was done right.

Vanity Fair was to be the first time that you learned my name and there would be the pictures. That couple of days of the shoot were the most fulfilling of my life. It was overwhelming. Annie was even crying at one point. My girl. I love Annie. The whole crew, the hair, the makeup, Jessica who did the styling, everybody really took it seriously because they knew the impact this could have on the marginalized trans world.

The cover was shot in my garage. We had to do everything in total secrecy. I had to put up walls around my house because the paparazzi were taking pictures from the surrounding mountains. We had security all over the mountains kicking people out.

I had this beautiful black off-the-shoulder Zac Posen dress that fit perfectly. Annie said, "Let's take a mirror and put it in behind the camera so you can see what we're trying to do here." I started crying. I had struggled for so long with identity, and that was the first time I looked in the mirror and liked what I saw. After it was over, the whole crew applauded.

The response was 99 per cent extraordinarily positive. And the article by Buzz Bissinger[1] was very important. He's a Pulitzer Prize-winning writer and was with me for three months writing that article. We did the book together.[2] The media kind of threw old Bruce under the bus, gone.

My biggest criticisms have been from the trans community. I got hammered for taking my appearance seriously. I get photographed every day, I try to dress properly. The trans community go: "What about all the people that can't do that, that don't have the money like this rich white girl to get things done that they need to get done? That's not representing our community." I think that, if you can present yourself in a positive manner where people are not uncomfortable around you, that helps everybody.

I am also criticized for being a conservative Republican. How can you be a conservative Republican and be trans? It's easy.

1   H G (Buzz) Bissinger, who wrote *Friday Night Lights* (Adison-Wesley, 1990), the story of a small town American football team, was chosen because he had a sports background and personal experience of cross-dressing.
2   Caitlyn Jenner, *The Secrets of My Life*, Trapeze, 2017.

ATTITUDE

JULY 2016

Editor: Matthew Todd
Art director: Peter Allison
Cover photographer: Leigh Kelly

A lifestyle monthly for gay men, British *Attitude* launched in 1994 and became famous for groundbreaking cover exclusives like David Beckham in 2002, when he was captain of England's national football team, and Tony Blair in 2005, the first time a serving British prime minister had spoken to a gay magazine. But this took it to another level. "The importance of a member of the royal family posing for the cover of a gay magazine for the first time cannot be overstated."[1]

MATTHEW TODD:

The cover has a lot to do with my experience of growing up as a gay man in the 1980s and feeling very alone. So to see Princess Diana then, even though she never explicitly said anything supportive of gay people, go to Mildmay Hospice, the HIV and AIDS hospice in London, and shake hands with people with AIDS was just incredible.

In 2012 I did a big feature on homophobic bullying and met quite a lot of parents of kids who'd been bullied. One young boy had killed himself. I did an interview with his father and, a few months later, he also took his own life.

I thought, "This is insane. Who could talk about this?" The royal family seemed like the obvious people. I wrote them a letter. These things take a long time but we started an ongoing discussion. Their Royal Highnesses are very keen not to be seen as celebrities. For them to engage with something, they have to have a genuine understanding of it.

In 2015 Prince William took part in a training session in Hammersmith about dealing with homophobic bullying as part of an initiative with the Diana Award. So, somewhere along the way, I like to think me writing to them may have provoked a genuine interest in the issue. Then, in early 2016, Kensington Palace agreed to the cover and invited us to bring some young LGBT people to tell Prince William what happened to them.

The focus of this cover and the feature inside was on LGBT mental health, because mental health is something that the Duke and Duchess are campaigning on. Their "Heads Together" campaign is something they're absolutely, totally, 100 per cent committed to. There are higher levels of addiction, anxiety, depression and suicide among LGBT people, so they wanted to engage with that.

We wanted to make sure that we had a really diverse mix of people, so we took a transgender person, a person who identifies as non-binary, two young gay black men, a young man who had an eating disorder, a lesbian woman who runs a youth project, a young Muslim man and Mena Houghton, the mother of a young gay man who died after years of homophobic bullying.

I've met prime ministers and superstars, but there's something very different about royalty. It might sound a bit crass but the only way to describe it is that it felt like there was a real sense of goodness about Prince William and an awareness of how he wanted to use his position. He genuinely wanted to help. Some of the young people were nervous so he was laughing and making jokes and telling us about how he'd been on the set of *Star Wars* to put us all at ease. He could not have been more charming. It was surreal.

It was my last issue as editor as well, so that was really great. I saw it as a very political cover. I was very aware that it would be seen all over the world, so we wanted to present a simple, stark message that would have impact. In the 1980s there was absolute savagery towards gay people; this is saying the opposite, that it's accepted and mainstream and that the highest figures in our society are supportive of it.

1 Matthew Todd, in interview with Ian Birch.

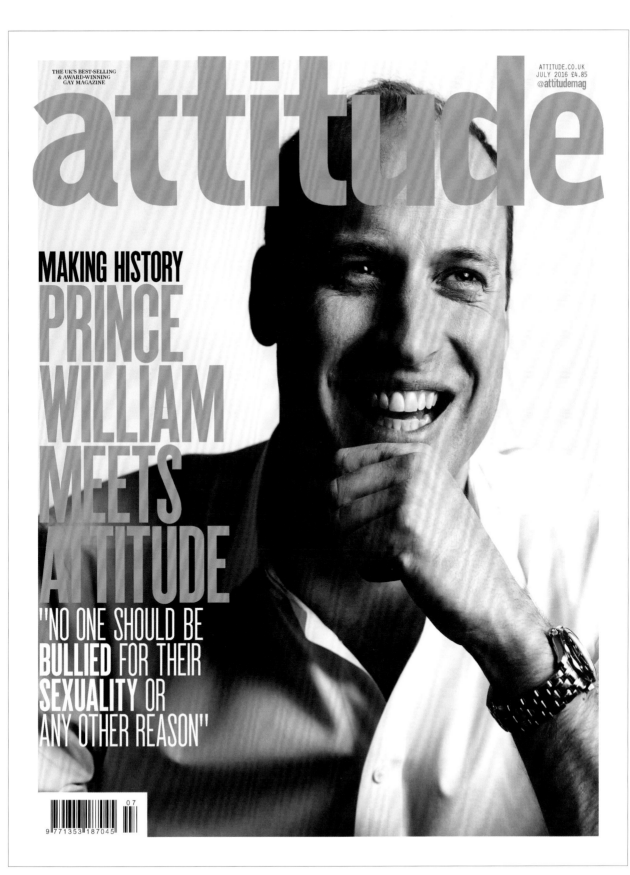

ATTITUDE.CO.UK
JULY 2016 £4.85
@attitudemag

attitude

MAKING HISTORY

PRINCE WILLIAM MEETS ATTITUDE

"NO ONE SHOULD BE **BULLIED** FOR THEIR **SEXUALITY** OR ANY OTHER REASON"

New York

July 27–Aug. 9, 2015

Alleged assault: ca. 1960s   In 1967   In 1969   In 1969   In 1969   In 1969   In 1969   Ca. 1970   Ca. 1970   Ca. 1970

In 1971   In 1973   In 1975   In 1975   In 1976   In 1977   In 1978 and 1980   In 1979   Ca. 1979   In 1981

In 1982   In 1982   In 1984   Ca. mid-1980s   Ca. mid-1980s   In 1985–87   In 1986   In 1986   In 1987   Ca. 1987

Ca. late 1980s   Ca. late 1980s   In 1989   Ca. early 1990s   In 1996

Cosby:
The Women

An Unwelcome Sisterhood

By Noreen Malone
A Portfolio by
Amanda Demme

NEW YORK

27 JULY–9 AUGUST 2015

Editor: Adam Moss
Design director: Thomas Alberty
Photography director: Jody Quon
Cover photographs: Amanda Demme
Cover story: Noreen Malone

In October 2014 a clip of stand-up comedian Hannibal Buress's routine in which he called Bill Cosby a rapist[1] went viral. This was not the first time "America's Dad"[2] had been accused of sexual misconduct. In 2005 ex-basketball star Andrea Constand made allegations against him, triggering a dozen women at the time to come forward with their own stories of assault.

The Buress clip galvanized more women to speak out; Cosby denied any wrongdoing. By the following July, there were 46 women, 35 of whom were willing to be photographed and interviewed for the magazine. In many ways, this cover presaged the "Me Too" movement that erupted two years later.

ADAM MOSS:

Jody felt very strongly that the Cosby accusers were not being taken seriously enough, and that there was an opportunity to gather as many of them as we could in one place, and to reframe the story in terms of the large numbers of people who had, one by one, come forward. She began against quite a bit of scepticism on my part that she'd be able to do this.

Very gradually, one person would say yes, and then another person, hearing that that person said yes, would do it. It took six months. There were a lot of reasons that they were reluctant to come forward. They were frightened. They weren't sure that they weren't somehow culpable. When we interviewed them, a lot of their feelings about their stories were quite the same.

JODY QUON:

I really couldn't believe it. I was a huge Cosby fan; I grew up with him. He was definitely a television role model. I went on the internet and made little dossiers of all the women who had come forward. I put them in chronological order by the year in which they said the incident happened. It went from the 1960s to basically the present. They were from all over the country and of every background and age. The list kept growing.

There was a little bit of resistance; no one could feel certain about how to evaluate the credibility of their stories. And this was also on the heels of the UVA *Rolling Stone* article.[3] I said, "Let me just cold call half a dozen of them." Six out of the six women that I found wanted their voices heard. They were so raw it was really moving.

Our strategy was to photograph the women in two different, unified colour schemes – black and white.[4] We didn't want the clothes to detract from who they were. Amanda, God bless her, came up with the idea to shoot them seated, feet on the ground, hands forward, ready. Almost like in a Western – "I'm ready for the duel."

AMANDA DEMME:

I wanted it to represent taking back power but in a very elegant way. It wouldn't have looked good in colour because every one of these ladies had a different tonality and the whole idea was that it had to look uniform. I am OCD. I have to have everything in straight lines, in grids. It's sort of military. I had everyone take off their jewellery, pretty much. And there was very little hair and make-up, and no mirrors so you could tszuj yourself. When they strip themselves of everything, they become super-powerful.

Most of them had never seen each other before and had never been in front of a professional photographer in their life. And they had a lot to say. They had been living with that secret for all those years. They felt so much anger but also hyper energy that they were finally going to be heard. I just said to them, look at me. You have to trust me. What I want everyone to see is your pain but not pity. You finally have your power.

In my presentation to the magazine, the empty chair was there just to show we had an uneven number and we needed one or three more people. But the magazine channelled my brain and turned that empty chair into an open seat. It was their time to have their voice and that's why it worked.

JODY QUON:

We didn't want any smiling for the whole portfolio. It was about empowerment. This was their moment, super-graphic. There was every emotion at every shoot

– crying, sadness, anger and then, at the end, exuberance. A sisterhood evolved. There was an incredible bonding, something we didn't even think to anticipate. Then the news broke of Andrea Constand in early July[5], and Adam decided to make it the cover.

ADAM MOSS:
"The Women" became the bold text and the word "Cosby" was done in this faint type, and was meant to very subtly give the ownership of the cover to the women. At sort of the last minute, we decided to do this chronologically and to insert the dates of the alleged assault. We had a chair that no one was in and the design director, Tom, just threw it on one version. We immediately understood the metaphor that it represented.

It became a hashtag, #theemptychair. Twelve thousand people participated (within the first 24 hours), and many of them described their own abuse stories, so it wasn't just about those people who had something to say about Bill Cosby. The empty chair became, in effect, what the whole story was about.

The impact was enormous. I've never seen a cover have as much of a public service role, per se. This was a piece of political activism. Ten more women came forward after this, and then it prompted various innovative legal strategies. Cosby didn't think he needed law enforcement at this point – because of the statute of limitations and various other things. Activist lawyers, newly enraged, devised new methods to bring some justice. The cover did, I think, reintroduce the case, and bring a kind of intensity to the consideration of it, and that's what I think a great cover can do. It can change a conversation.

1 Buress said: "He [Cosby] gets on TV, 'Pull your pants up black people, I was on TV in the 80s! I can talk down to you because I had a successful sitcom!' Yeah, but you rape women, Bill Cosby, so turn the crazy down a couple notches."
2 His role as Dr Cliff Huxtable in the 1980s hit sitcom *The Cosby Show* turned him into a cultural icon.
3 Sabrina Erdely, "A Rape on Campus", *Rolling Stone*, 12 November 2014. The magazine retracted the article, about an alleged group sexual assault by fraternity members at the University of Virginia (UVA), in April the following year.
4 These appear in the feature inside.
5 In 2005 Constand brought a civil case against Cosby, accusing him of drugging and molesting her. He defended himself in a deposition which was unsealed ten years later by a federal judge in Philadelphia on Monday 6 July 2015.

TIME

Meltdown.

TIME

22 AUGUST 2016
24 OCTOBER 2016

Managing editor: Nancy Gibbs
Design director: D W Pine III
Director of photography & visual enterprise:
  Kira Pollack
Cover illustrations: Edel Rodriguez

As soon as the July National Conventions were over, Donald Trump went on an extraordinary tear. He lashed out at the parents of a Muslim American soldier killed on duty in Iraq; he called President Barack Obama the "founder of ISIS". The Republican Party seemed in turmoil. *Time* responded with the "Meltdown" cover. Then, on 7 October, the *Washington Post* released a video showing Trump and TV host Billy Bush engaged in a crass conversation from 2005. *Time* responded with "Total Meltdown". As Mike Lupica commented: "You put those two covers together and it looks like he's the Wicked Witch of the West. He's shrinking and melting at the same time."[1] Rodriguez distils Trump into what he calls a "simple branding device" of lurid yellow hair, orange skin and braying mouth, which he has subsequently developed for more coruscating covers of *Time* and *Der Spiegel*. "He (Trump) loves *Time* magazine," Rodriguez later commented. "That's my main pleasure, knowing that these people are looking at it and it's ruining their day."[2] Many of Rodriguez's anti-Trump drawings appear on placards in street protests. He has made the artwork downloadable for this purpose.

EDEL RODRIGUEZ:

With the first Trump, everybody needed to vent. It had been a year of putting up with this nonsense, this awful human, and finally someone made an image. I just happened to be the person that delivered it. And it wasn't in an indie like the *Village Voice*. It was in *Time*. About 50 per cent of the problem is to get a big publication like *Time* to have the guts to publish something like that.

D W PINE III:

It was a Friday and Michael Scherer, our Washington bureau chief, was on the phone, talking about Trump. He said, "It seems like he's just melting down." I thought, "That's a visual." I talked to Edel over the weekend and he came back with a couple of versions.

On Monday our concern was, "Were we being fair? Was Meltdown too much?" On Tuesday there was another Trump blunder so we thought, "We're fine."

The challenge with the illustration was to make it look like Trump. Obviously, the orangey skin and those gold locks of hair help, but what did it for me was the simplicity of his mouth – open, and talking emphatically, no matter what, as the drips come down his face.

EDEL RODRIGUEZ:

That image is like a one-liner. If you're going to throw one-liners at me, I'm going to throw a one-liner at you. A good magazine cover should be able to take a complicated matter and communicate it directly to as many people as possible. I try to make something simple that speaks over a long term.

It's important to provoke a feeling, but if you just have a feeling without any intellectual backing, that's propaganda and I don't want to do that. I come from Cuba and grew up surrounded by meaningless political posters.

D W PINE III:

The Trump–Billy Bush incident enflamed everybody here. The focus of our story was how Trump was debasing his own party. I asked Edel if he wanted to take the GOP's elephant logo and do a similar kind of dripping treatment with it. Then, our story became more about how Trump was really going off the rails, especially when you compared him to a traditional candidate. But we don't live in traditional times. I said to Edel, "Why don't we have him completely melting down?" Within about a couple of hours, we came up with "Total Meltdown".

Trump never commented about these covers and yet he has on almost every other cover we have done. The "Total Meltdown" cover went on to win the ASME[3] cover of the year.

1   Mike Lupica on *Morning Joe*, MSNBC, 13 October 2016. Lupica is an author and columnist for the *New York Daily News* and an MSNBC contributor.
2   Katharine Schwab, "Meet The Preeminent Illustrator of the Trump Era", 16 January 2018. https://amp. fastcodesign.com/90157026/meet-the-preeminent-illustrator-of-the-trump-era?__twitter_impression=true
3   The American Society of Magazine Editors.

TIME

Total
Meltdown.

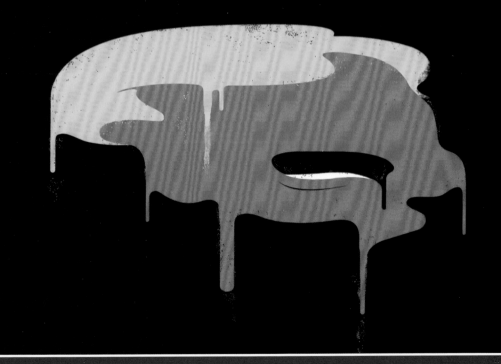

PRIVATE EYE

11–24 NOVEMBER 2016

Editor: Ian Hislop

Shortly after Gina Miller and Deir Dos Santos launched a legal challenge to the British government about triggering Article 50, which would start the countdown for the country to leave the European Union, *Private Eye* published this cover. There was an avalanche of frenzied complaints. One reader wanted to "shove our smug opinions so far up our asses that we choked our guts out – which was sort of charming in its way".[1] Another, a vicar, "told me it was time to accept the victory of the majority of the people and to stop complaining. Acceptance is a virtue, he said. I wrote back and told him this argument was a bit much coming from a church that had begun with a minority of twelve. Or you could say with a minority of one on Good Friday when all the others ran away."[2]

IAN HISLOP:

Nev Fountain and Tom Jamieson, two of our writers, came in with the bus fully formed. They had a yellow bus and I changed it to a decaying red bus just to match the pictures up. The bus was rusting in a field somewhere up in, I think, northern Scotland. It was a brilliant metaphor – the old music hall joke, the wheels have come off the bus, but done with the original Brexit bus with the big lie on the side. This is literally as the Brexit process runs into the sand.

It was a very, very striking cover, but it was a very, very annoying cover for a huge number of people who wrote in and said they thought we were attacking the Health Service or various things like that, but it was pretty clear what it was about. They were very cross indeed. I think there were certainly some people who've come to politics a bit late, or they've come to being passionate about politics a bit late, and usually with a single cause like Scottish nationalism – or they joined UKIP.[3] They're outraged that anyone disagrees with them, and outraged that anyone should laugh. Everything is so polarized and I think social media has made people ruder and less tolerant and less willing to argue the case, rather than just state an opinion or say, "It should be banned."

You can't just ban everyone you don't like. That's not really how it works. And, again, if you've won the election or you've won the referendum, that doesn't mean everyone has to shut up for ever. The argument goes on – that's the other bit of democracy.

1 Ian Hislop, "The Right to Dissent (and the Left Too)", George Orwell Lecture 2016, University College London, 15 November 2016.

2 Ibid.

3 The right-wing, populist UK Independence Party, which since its foundation in 1993 campaigned for UK withdrawal from the EU.

PRIVATE EYE

No. 1431
11 November –
24 Nov 2016
£1.80

BREXIT LATEST

THEN

NOW

INDEX

PICTURE CREDITS

ACKNOWLEDGEMENTS

First, a big thank you to everybody I interviewed for your participation, enthusiasm and, of course, for letting me tell your stories.

Unless credited to other sources, all the quotes come from interviews I did throughout 2016 and 2017. With One, all the major protagonists had died so I talked to Craig M Loftin, Lecturer in American Studies at California State University, Fullerton, who has written widely about the period and the magazine.

For advice, support, insights, contacts and access to personal archives, a second big thank you to Jaap Biemans, Mark Blackwell, Marissa Bourke, Cath Caldwell, David Carey, Nicholas Coleridge, Ian Denning, Mark Ellen, Simon Esterson, Malcolm Garrett, Chris Heath, Suzanne Hodgart, Andrew Hussey, James Hyman, Richard Morton Jack, Jeremy Leslie, Mark Lewisohn, Shari Kaufman, Terry Mansfield, Terence Pepper, Jane Pluer, Marcus Rich, Kathy Ryan, Dave Rimmer, David Robson, Jon Savage, Jim Seymore, Peter Steinfels, Suzanne Sykes, Neil Tennant, Craig Tomashoff, Michael Watts, Fred Woodward and Wendy Wolf.

A third big thank you to my agent Juliet Pickering, Damian Horner who started the ball rolling, and the folks at Octopus: Pauline Bache, Joe Cottington, Sophie Hartley, Giulia Hetherington and Hannah Knowles.

The biggest thanks must go to my family – to my sons, William for his original thinking, and Matthew for his steady encouragement, but most of all to my wife, Markie, without whose support, understanding and copy skills this book would never have seen the light of day.

A FIREFLY BOOK

Published by Firefly Books Ltd. 2018

Text copyright © 2018 Ian Birch
Design and layout copyright © 2018
  Octopus Publishing Group

First printing

Publisher Cataloging-in-Publication Data (U.S.)

Library of Congress Control Number: 2018941267

Library and Archives Canada Cataloguing in Publication

Birch, Ian, 1950-, author
     Iconic magazine covers : the inside stories told by the people who made them / Ian Birch.
Includes bibliographical references and index.
ISBN 978-0-228-10117-8 (hardcover)
     1. Magazine covers--History--20th century.
2. Magazine covers--History--21st century. I. Title.
NC974.B57 2018   741.6'52   C2018-902203-5

Published in the United States by
Firefly Books (U.S.) Inc.
P.O. Box 1338, Ellicott Station
Buffalo, New York 14205

Published in Canada by
Firefly Books Ltd.
50 Staples Avenue, Unit 1
Richmond Hill, Ontario L4B 0A7

Printed in China

First published by Cassell,
a division of Octopus Publishing Group Ltd
Carmelite House
50 Victoria Embankment
London EC4Y 0DZ

Ian Birch asserts the moral right to be identified
as the author of this work.
Commissioning editors Hannah Knowles
and Joe Cottington
Senior editor Pauline Bache
Senior designer Jaz Bahra
Picture research manager Giulia Hetherington
Picture researcher Sophie Hartley
Typesetter Ed Pickford
Copyeditor Robert Anderson
Senior production manager Katherine Hockley